AF896468

THE VISUAL DATA LANGUAGE

THE KNIME WAY

DENNIS GANZAROLI

To my loving wife Beatrice, whose unwavering support and faith in me have been my constant source of strength throughout this journey.

To my parents, who gave me the values of curiosity, perseverance, and a lifelong passion for learning.

To my former mentors, Josef Schmid, Ole Vossnack and Dani Meyer, whose guidance and wisdom shaped my path in Data Science and beyond.

And to Rosaria Silipo, ever-energetic evangelist of KNIME, who always believed in me and supported me.

Thank you for inspiring me to reach new heights!

FOREWORD

When I first discovered the power of data, I was sitting in a movie theater watching **Back to the Future Part II.**

Like many others, I was fascinated by the DeLorean time machine. But what really inspired me was not the car or the flux capacitor, but a little book: **Gray's Sports Almanac**.

With this book, Biff Tannen could predict the outcome of all major sporting events for decades and become rich.

Building a real time machine? That was pure fantasy. Even after a semester of physics, I knew that bending time was beyond reach. But what if there was another way to see into the future - not through science fiction, but with the help of data?

During my psychology studies, I did my internship at a market research company and took my first steps into the world of data. What I discovered was fascinating: Data not only records the past, but often contains **hidden patterns** that can be used to **make predictions**.

I didn't travel through time, but I began to see how the future is formed through data. This moment was the birth of my journey into the world of data and data science.

Nevertheless, I didn't (yet) get rich with sports betting, but thanks to my experience with data, I was able to get very good jobs and earn good money in my 25 years as a **data specialist**.

More importantly, I gained a powerful skill: the ability to turn data into insight and insight into action.

This book shows my journey into the world of data and how to use a visual programming language like **KNIME** to master all the challenges of working with data.

I hope you enjoy reading this book and that it inspires you with new great ideas.

May the Data Force be with you!

CONTENTS

INTRODUCTION

In this introduction to **Data Science**, we will take a different approach than usual. Instead of diving straight into theories and formulas, we will take a practical approach. Therefore, we will first focus on the **working tool** and the advantages of a **visual programming language**.

Since a large part of data science consists of **data engineering**, mastering this skill is essential. Learning a visual programming language like **KNIME** not only makes it easier to get started but also proves to be an important cornerstone for the entire path of data science.

With more than **25 years of experience** in data science, working for different companies in different sectors and with different data tools, I can assure you that having the right tool is essential.

We will set up the necessary tools and a freely accessible **data science infrastructure** that fully meets the technical requirements of real-world applications, all without any additional software costs.

KNIME has been the **best kept secret in data science** for years. It quietly enables people to do serious work. If you work with data, you will understand why: it works. It's **open source**, runs on all major platforms, and allows you to build workflows without writing a single line of code.

At the same time, it doesn't limit you. You can integrate **Python, R, SQL**, or even **machine learning** models whenever needed. What makes it stand out is the way it brings different roles together. **Business analysts, data engineers,**

and scientists can work together in the same environment, following the same logic.

That kind of consistency is rare. With KNIME, you're not locked into a specific language or method. You focus on **solving problems**. The rest gets out of the way.

In the final part of the book, you'll find **real data examples** that put **KNIME in Action**. These practical cases demonstrate how different kinds of problems can be solved using KNIME, from data preparation to analysis and reporting. They illustrate how KNIME is applied to solve real-life problems.

Having the right tools is essential, but they alone won't guarantee success - you also need the necessary **motivation** to see it through. And even with the motivation, learning by itself won't suffice.

To truly succeed, you need to dive into the process with passion - you must live it and love it! No one can do it for you. Only through experience, dedication, and curiosity can you truly succeed.

Trust me, if your goal is to become a data scientist, you must change your **hobbies**!

1

THE KNIME WAY

Data is everywhere in our interconnected global world, touching nearly every aspect of our lives - from the groceries we buy to the websites we visit and the opinions we express.

As data's importance continues to grow, organizations increasingly rely on it to better understand their customers, optimize promotions, and achieve much more. Business and data analysts have become the driving force behind addressing complex business questions.

However, many analysts struggle to meet these new challenges because traditional tools and methods are no longer sufficient. Using spreadsheets such as Excel, manual processes and custom scripts is proven to be too time consuming and tedious, especially given the volume of ad hoc requests the analysts receive daily. At the same time, management expectations are rising steadily, driven by intensifying market competition.

What is Data Blending?

Data blending differs from **data integration** in that it focuses on addressing specific use cases, whereas data integration typically aims to create a unified "single source of truth" stored in a data warehouse for broad access.

Traditional data integration processes involve extracting data from multiple databases, transforming it into a normalized format suitable for analysis, and loading it into a data warehouse. Business analysts can then explore this consolidated data using advanced analytical tools such as **MicroStrategy**, **Tableau** or **Power BI**.

Data blending is the process of collecting data from multiple sources and merging it into one easily consumable dataset for further analysis.

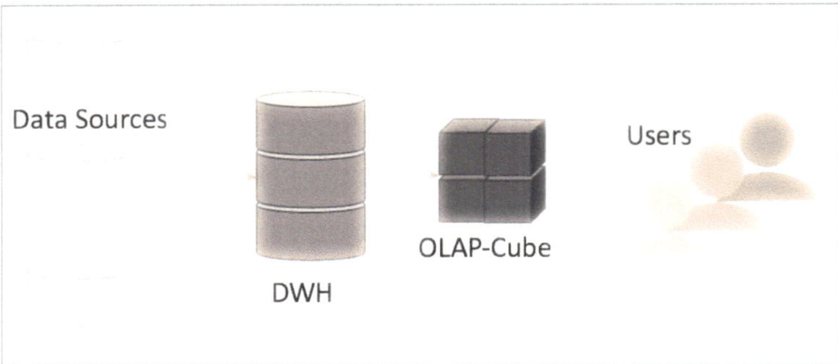

Fig. 1.1 Data Blending

The goal is to extract valuable information to help for example leaders to make better decisions.

The challenge with this approach is that it is managed by the **IT department** rather than business analysts. While this ensures the process is industrialized, scheduled, and centrally governed, it lacks flexibility.

What happens when an analyst urgently needs to combine data sources? IT cannot design and execute a new process for every ad-hoc request. In a tightly packed roadmap or **Program Increment** (PI) planning cycle, there is little room to accommodate such on-the-fly needs.

So, what are the alternatives for the business analyst to achieve his goals within the set deadlines?

Learning the right thing

I remember years ago when a friend of mine took a training course in **Visual Basic for Applications** (VBA) to improve his programming skills and speed up his workflows. He spent five days and around $3,000 learning the basics of the scripting language.

Did it help him tackle his data blending tasks more efficiently? Not at all. Instead, he became overwhelmed with self-doubt and frustration, and his problems stayed unsolved.

Finally, he asked me if I could help him with VBA. I gave it a try but quickly realized it wasn't the best fit for his needs, so I suggested **KNIME** (https://www.knime.com/) instead.

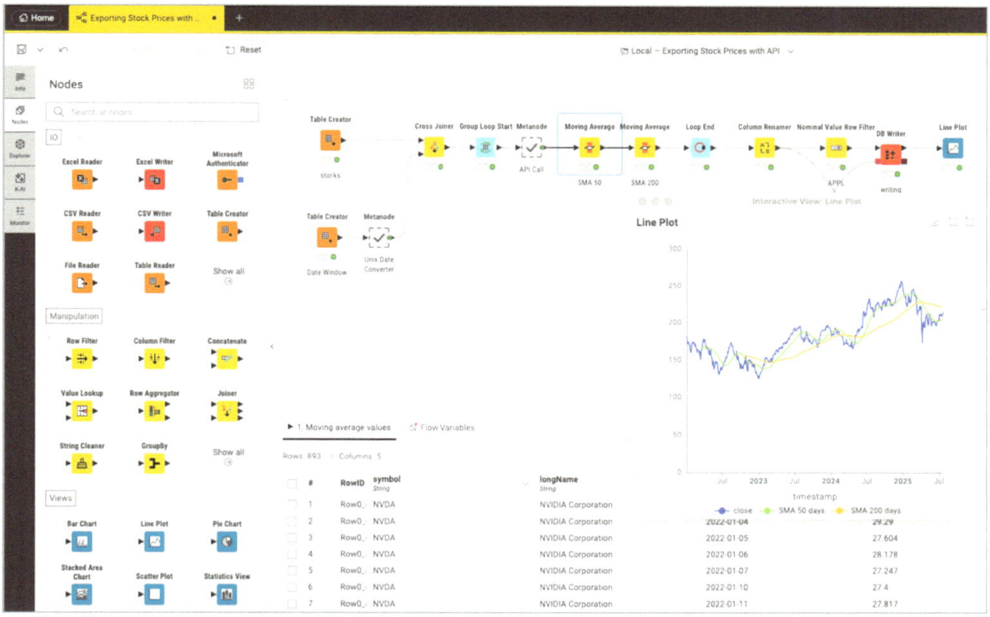

Fig. 1.2 KNIME is an open-source software for data science

Since his department didn't have the budget for a SAS or SPSS Modeler license, KNIME, being open-source, was the perfect alternative.

Although starting from scratch without formal training seemed daunting to him, he managed to solve his task in just a week. He proudly showed me his solution, and from that moment on, his work pace improved dramatically.

A visual-based GUI tool can be learned and applied much faster than a script-based programming language, allowing users to save valuable time and resources for more critical analyses and investigations

Let's go back to the beginning: it was the 1990s, and I had just started my studies when, during a computer science lecture, I encountered a programming language that captivated me from the start.

That language was **Prograph for Mac**.

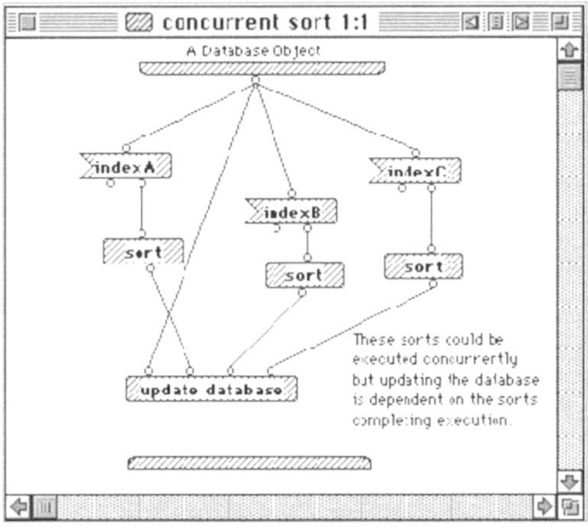

Fig. 1.3 Prograph for Mac (image from Wikipedia)

Prograph was incredibly intuitive and far less prone to the syntax issues commonly found in textual programming languages. I immediately recognized its potential, particularly for applications in data analysis. At the time, I had just begun writing my first research papers, which required extensive data analysis.

A few years later, my dreams came true when, in 1994, **SPSS** introduced the first version of **Clementine**, now known as **IBM SPSS Modeler**.

This was a complete game-changer. For the first time, users could load data from Excel or CSV files or query it directly from various databases using SQL, all without the need for coding.

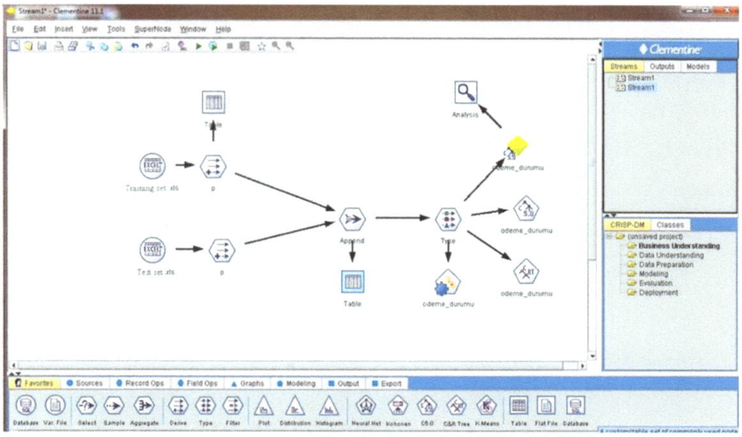

Fig. 1.4 SPSS-Clementine 11.1

Business analysts were suddenly empowered to build **data pipelines** (workflows) and even create predictive models - at the time referred to as data mining models - simply by dragging and dropping dedicated blocks (nodes) within a graphical user interface (GUI).

Each node performed a specific task, such as filtering rows, grouping data, or joining datasets, as illustrated in the image.

A workflow replaced an entire script, with each node representing one or more lines of code. Step by step, the pipeline was built, configured, executed, inspected, and documented seamlessly. Moreover, the workflows were reusable, saving time and eliminating the need to start from scratch for every project.

However, there was a significant drawback: the licenses were prohibitively expensive. This prompted a crucial question: how could one gain access to the software? The common solution was to work for a company that already held the necessary licenses. But what if your company couldn't afford them? Would you still be able to deliver results?

License costs are of vital importance!

If you can't afford the software, you won't be able to deliver. Therefore, open-source solutions are often the better alternative. While the tool may not have the most modern GUI, the support of a large community ensures that your work is built on a solid foundation.

Reasons for KNIME

I had several great years working with Clementine. In 2004, while working at SPSS, I came across KNIME - a tool similar to Clementine but open-source and therefore accessible to everyone. Excited about its potential, I shared my discovery with my boss at the time. To my surprise, he already knew about it but quickly silenced me, making it clear that no one should talk about it.

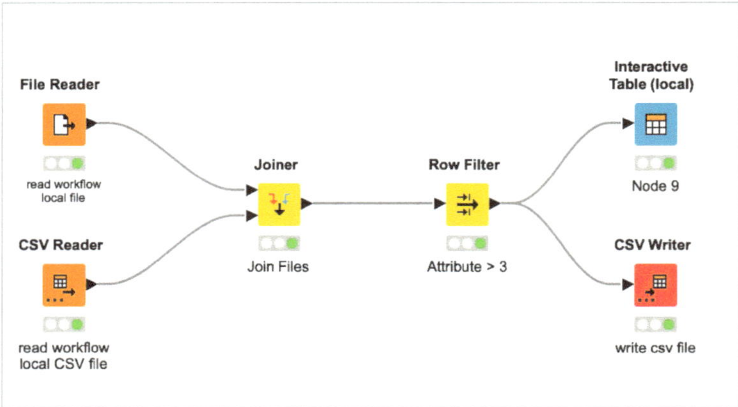

Fig. 1.5 A typical KNIME workflow: Loading and joining data

Years later, at a different company, I joined a newly created business unit. Although it was a large company, there was no budget for data blending tools like SPSS Modeler or SAS for that unit. I decided to revisit KNIME, but this time in a productive environment.

Ten years have passed since then, and I can safely say that this was one of the best decisions of my professional career. But what made this choice so successful? Here are the key reasons:

1.) Automating Repetitive Tasks

Our business analysts primarily worked with **MicroStrategy**, exporting data to Excel for further processing. While they excelled at manipulating data in Excel, the increasing volume and diversity of data quickly exceeded their capabilities.

Tasks as simple as merging two datasets became a nightmare, and transforming columns in Excel turned unexpectedly complicated in some cases. The most frustrating challenge arose when a file format changed, causing everything in Excel to break. We needed a new approach to tackle these issues.

KNIME's visual programming language proved to be the perfect solution. It is intuitive, self-explanatory, and easy to learn, enabling our business analysts to become productive with the tool in no time. After just a few weeks of practice, they were confidently using KNIME with minimal assistance and improving their workflows.

2.) Sourcing Data from Anywhere

Accessing a data warehouse via SQL is undoubtedly one of the fastest ways to retrieve the data you need, but it's not always an option. At times, building a new API or addressing other technical restrictions may be required - but management often doesn't have the time to wait for such implementations.

In these cases, you sometimes must opt for manual methods, such as exporting data from front-end tools like Salesforce, SAP or MicroStrategy and importing it into KNIME for further processing. Even if this approach is not the most elegant, it is often the most practical and effective solution.

Although the initial step of manually exporting the data can be tedious, everything after that can be automated and executed quickly. For weekly or monthly reports, this workflow is usually more than sufficient to meet the demands.

3.) Easy Documentation and Collaboration

A well-documented workflow can be a lifesaver, especially if the workflow's owner is on vacation and your boss urgently needs results. What makes good documentation?

The best documentation is often one that isn't even necessary - where the workflow itself is so well-structured and intuitive that its purpose and logic are immediately clear. (Of course, people can sometimes create chaotic workflows, and not even KNIME can fix that!)

This clarity also enhances collaboration. Tasks can easily be divided into smaller, reusable components and later reassembled. This ensures that everyone involved has a shared understanding of the workflow, making teamwork smoother and more efficient.

4.) Automating Workflows

There comes a point when weekly reports are no longer sufficient, and management demands daily updates on business performance. Meanwhile, IT has built the API, allowing you to directly source data from the warehouse.

With KNIME, you can create a workflow to extract, transform, and report this data automatically - running every morning at a fixed time.

With **KNIME Business Hub**, this process is seamless. You design a workflow and publish it from the KNIME Client to the KNIME Business Hub using drag-and-drop, and then schedule it for regular execution. Once the workflow completes, you receive an email notification, and the data or report is ready for review.

This automation not only ensures timely delivery of reports but also frees up employees to focus on more analytical and strategic tasks.

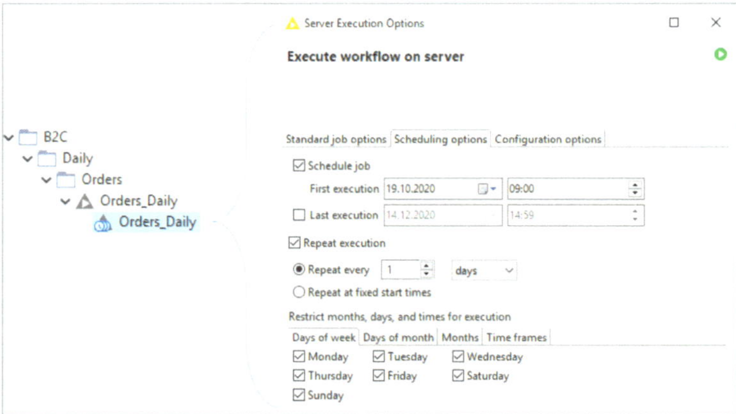

Fig. 1.6 Scheduled workflows on the KNIME Business Hub

In our team, we call our KNIME Business Hub our "robot colleague" because it constantly saves us time and streamlines our processes.

5.) A Scalable Platform for Everyone and Every Use Case

Not every employee possesses the same skill set, and their responsibilities can differ significantly. For instance, while a business analyst may primarily focus on merging and processing data from spreadsheets, a data scientist often delves into building advanced predictive models.

Data scientists frequently rely on languages like R and Python, known for their robust libraries tailored to various data science tasks. KNIME seamlessly integrates with Python, enabling users to embed their scripts directly into workflows. The same flexibility extends to R and JavaScript. A standout feature is KNIME's ability to call Jupyter notebooks directly within its environment, eliminating the need for a separate Jupyter Server.

6.) LLMs and Generative AI Integration

The latest advancements in KNIME have introduced integration with large language models (LLMs) and Generative AI, transforming how data professionals and domain experts tackle complex tasks.

For instance, users can now leverage LLMs for text analysis and summarization, allowing them to process vast amounts of unstructured text data and extract meaningful insights or generate concise summaries. This capability simplifies working with text-heavy datasets.

Another transformative feature is the ability to create conversational agents, such as **chatbots** or virtual assistants, directly within KNIME workflows.

Through integration - either via APIs from leading providers such as **OpenAI**, **Hugging Face**, or **DeepSeek**, or locally via **ChatGPT4All** - users can build intelligent systems for customer service, internal support, or interactive applications.

KNIME also streamlines workflow creation through automated code generation. **KNIME AI (K-AI)**, a feature leveraging advanced AI capabilities, can draft Python or R scripts, configure KNIME nodes, or even generate detailed documentation based on task descriptions. This functionality reduces the time and expertise needed to design robust solutions, making advanced workflows more accessible to all users.

Finally, KNIME facilitates enhanced predictive modeling by enabling hybrid solutions that combine traditional predictive techniques with the power of LLMs. For example, users can forecast sales trends while simultaneously generating detailed business narratives to support their findings.

These capabilities make KNIME an even more versatile and powerful tool, enabling organizations to expand their use cases and achieve deeper insights with the support of cutting-edge generative AI technologies.

With over **2,000 native nodes** and a vast array of extensions, KNIME provides comprehensive support for virtually every aspect of data science. From tasks like text mining and big data processing to the integration of cutting-edge AI technologies, KNIME empowers users to handle the entire data journey. Whether it's gathering and cleaning data, building sophisticated models, creating insightful visualizations, or implementing advanced artificial intelligence solutions, KNIME offers a scalable and versatile platform for a wide range of analytical requirements.

2

LEARNING A VISUAL PROGRAMMING LANGUAGE

The "Excel-Filter"

I call it the **Excel-Filter**: more and more companies hiring **data engineers** are automatically rejecting candidates who include Excel as a skill on their CV. For decades, Excel was the gold standard for **business analysts** and controllers.

However, in today's complex data-driven world - where seamless integration and analysis across multiple datasets is essential - Excel alone no longer makes the cut.

Fig. 2.1 The Excel-Filter

The demands on **data engineers** have become even more rigorous. They must efficiently combine diverse data sources from different systems and enable automated, real-time analysis.

Gone are the days when management was content with weekly or monthly reports. Today, data needs to be accessible at least daily, ideally in real-time, because time has become an even more critical asset than ever before. Traditional spreadsheet tools like Excel are no longer sufficient for managing the complexity of modern workflows.

While Python can handle most technical tasks, it falls short when it comes to collaboration among team members with diverse expertise or maintaining clear documentation. Therefore, a different approach is needed.

Learning a **visual programming language** (VPL) instead of **Python** can enable you to solve 99% of your data engineering tasks. My former team, which I led as Head of Report and Data Management, continues to work effectively with KNIME and some SQL. I would argue they have always been more efficient and productive than the Python specialists in that organization.

Their progress was remarkably fast. When I took over the team, they only knew Excel. After a three-day KNIME course, they were up and running, and within just a few weeks, they were already delivering results.

Okay, not everyone is going to make it that fast. You must have a certain disposition.

People who naturally think in pictures often have an edge here. People generally process information in one of two main ways: either through words or through images. Visual thinkers tend to understand and organize information more easily when it is presented in a visual format such as diagrams, charts, or mind maps. In contrast, those who think more verbally usually prefer information in the form of written or spoken language.

You can often spot this difference immediately when you show someone a **mind map**, like the one in the next image.

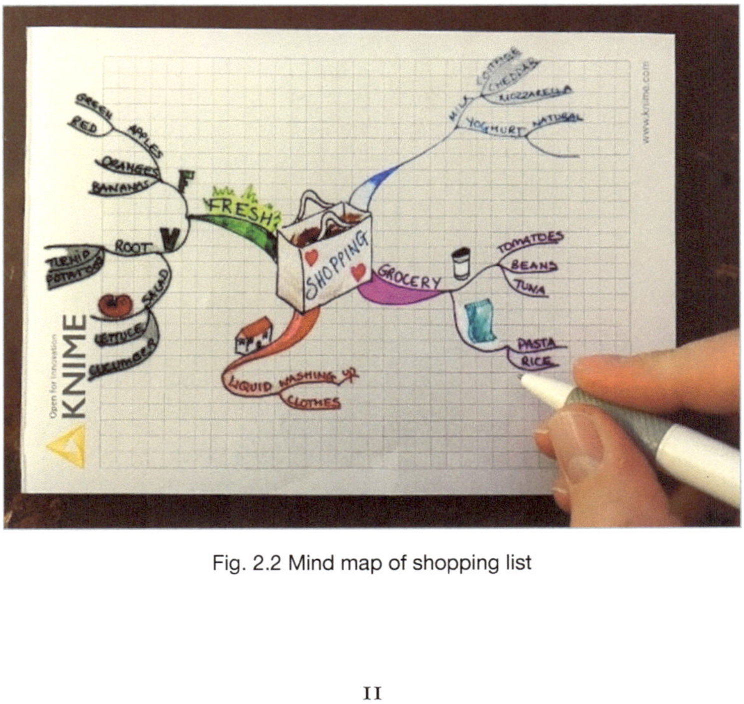

Fig. 2.2 Mind map of shopping list

People who think visually will find this map more intuitive and engaging, while those who think in words may prefer a straightforward list like the one in the next image.

Fig. 2.3 Shopping list

They tend to prefer a linear sequence of tasks to complete, rather than exploring holistic connections between topics. This reflects a more action-oriented mindset. It quickly becomes clear that we're also dealing with different personality types here.

Why is "Visual Programming" a language?

Typically, we associate a language with written text, but not all languages rely on an alphabetical system. Linguists classify written languages according to various **writing systems**. In addition to alphabetic systems, many cultures like Chinese and Japanese use logographic systems.

In languages like Chinese and Japanese, logographic writing uses symbols (or glyphs) to represent whole words or morphemes - meaningful units of language - rather than individual sounds or letters.

But why did I end up with the hieroglyphs now? Maybe because when my wife saw me working with KNIME for the first time, she said to me:

> „What are you doing with these hieroglyphs?"

She intuitively understood that I was dealing with a writing system for the ETL-process.

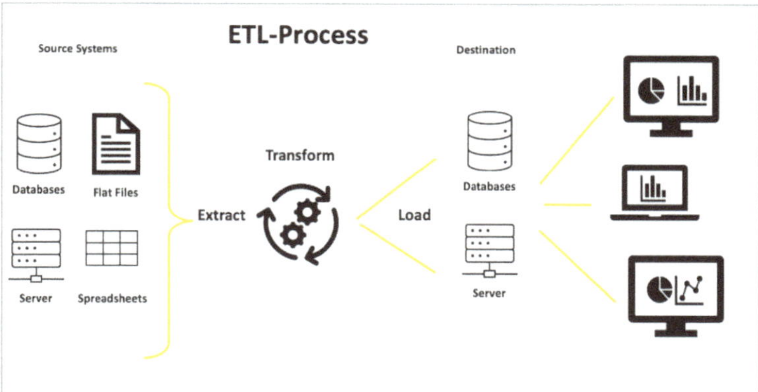

Fig. 2.4 The ETL process

ETL is a type of data integration that refers to the three phases (extract, transform, and load) that are used to combine data from various sources. Data is extracted from different source systems, transformed into an analyzable format, and loaded into a data warehouse or other system.

The best representation of an ETL pipeline is a visual workflow.

Judge it for yourself: Which of the following two representations is closest to the process above? The one on the left or the one on the right?

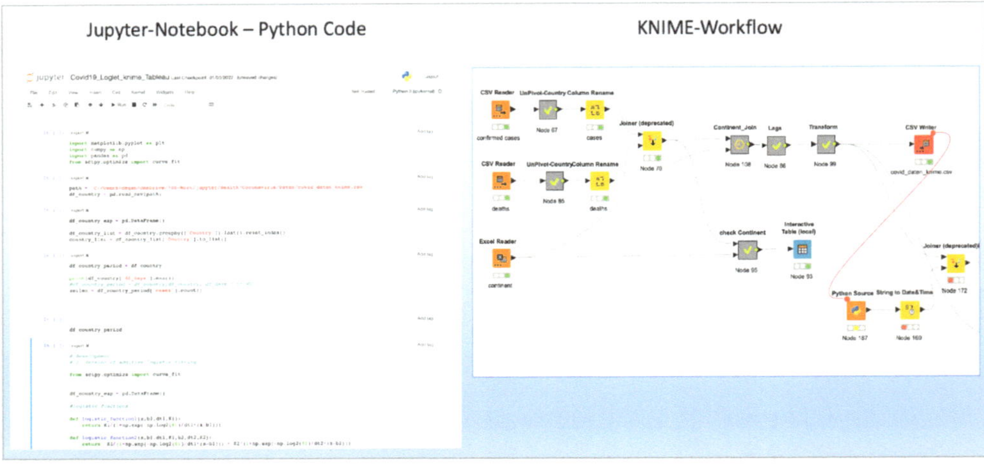

Fig. 2.5 Python script vs KNIME Workflow

The visual environment provides just the right amount of abstraction to build and share your work. Yes, because you will always be working with others and therefore need to be able to document and share your work.

Nowadays no data scientist or data engineer works alone anymore.

We are all part of teams, and we all need to communicate together. Discussion of the tasks, best practices, documentation are all necessary tasks in the daily work.

Documentation is an important part of collaboration, and therefore a common language is necessary to enable communication and understanding to both, data engineers and business stakeholders. After you have learned to work with a VPL, you will sometimes hear the following story from your teammates:

> „Hey, remember when we used to work with Excel?
> Feels like ages ago!“

The words of a Visual Programming Language

KNIME Analytics Platform implements visual programming. This means that each data transformation step is represented by means of an **icon block**, called a **node**, in a graphical editor.

Each node can perform one specific task. For example, in the figure below the **File Reader** node reads a CSV file and the **Row Filter** node allows to filter rows based on a filter criterion.

In the example, we load the sales records and filter them to include only those from Germany. Then we write our selection into an Excel file.

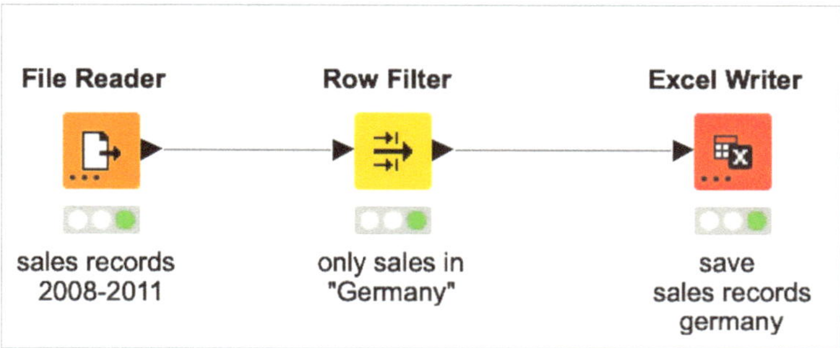

Fig. 2.6 Different nodes for every data transformation step

A sequence of connected nodes is called a **workflow** and is the corresponding concept of a programming code e.g., in Python or other programming languages.

As shown in the next image, the ETL process consists of three main components:

Input -> Transform -> Output

Fig. 2.7 The three main basic components of an ETL-process

The task of the **input** is to load different data source types into the processing tool. In **KNIME** there are several nodes available that allow to load data, both from a CSV or an Excel-file to any table from any database.

Fig. 2.8 Data Access nodes in KNIME

At the **output**, the data is exported back to other databases, systems, or files.

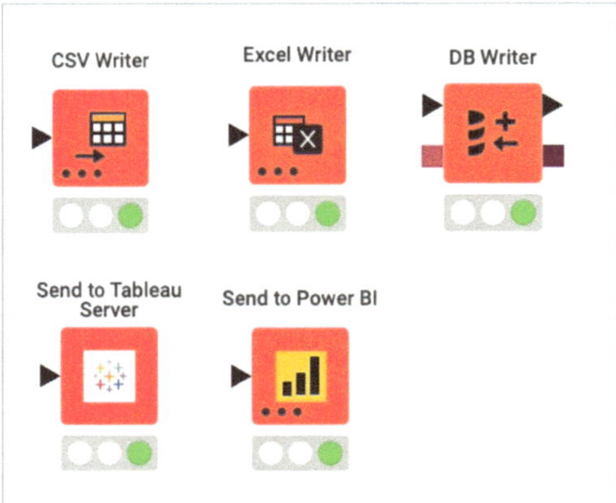

Fig. 2.9 Data Writer nodes in KNIME

In KNIME we have the choice between exporting to a CSV file, to an Excel file, writing the data to a database, or even to BI visualization tools like **Tableau** or **Power BI** for further analysis.

The **transformation** process, on the other hand, can be divided into further sub-processes:

1.) Transforming

a) Functions (Mathematical and Text functions)

You can create columns in a data table by applying a function to existing columns. This function can be a **mathematical** or a **text function**. In KNIME there are several dedicated nodes for this purpose. The result is a new column created from one or more columns.

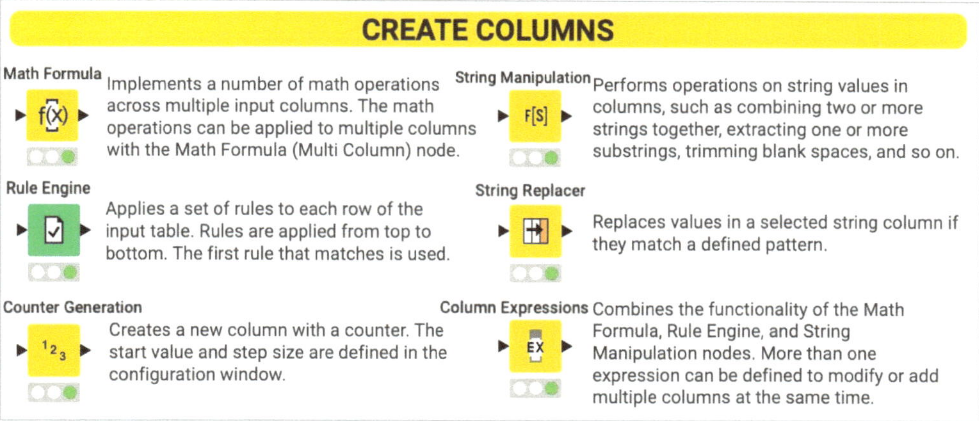

Fig. 2.10 Create new columns with functions

b) Filtering (Rows and Columns)

In KNIME there is no difference between filtering and removing rows, as the original table is not deleted and is still available at the output of the previous node. And that is a very important key point for reusability. You just need to adjust the filter node to your needs, and the workflow is ready to use again.

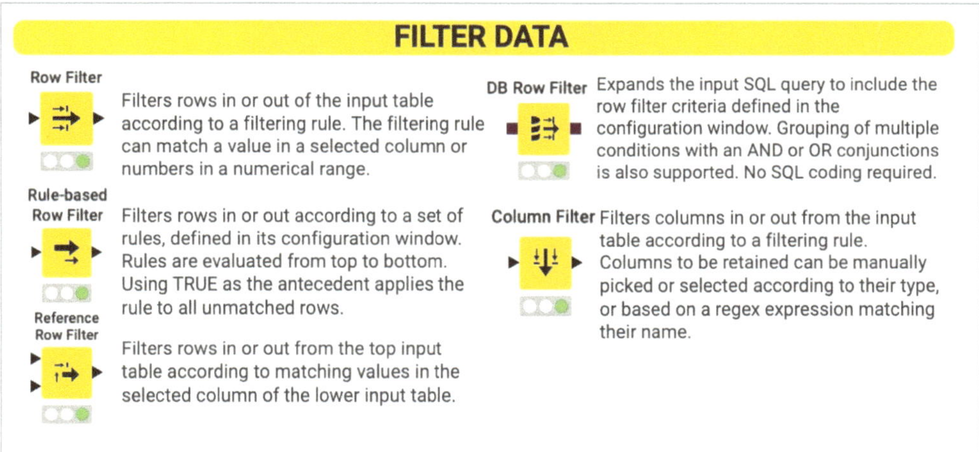

Fig. 2.11 Filter data in KNIME

In our previous example: if you want to select sales records of France instead of Germany, you just need to change the filter node, and the data will be available again since nothing has been deleted.

2. Aggregate and Reshape

a) Group By

This function is known from SQL and is used to group together any rows of a column with the same value stored in them, based on a function specified in the configuration of the node. Generally, these functions are one of the aggregate functions such as maximum(), sum() and avg().

For example, you have daily weight values from different people and want to display the maximum and average values for every person in a table.

Fig. 2.12 Aggregate data with the GroupBy function

In KNIME we can choose from over 30 aggregation functions. This helps to get things done faster and more efficiently. And just like in any other node, the parameters can be adjusted and reused without having to start all over again.

b) Pivoting

The **Pivoting** node is a further enhancement of the **GroupBy** node. It is a combination of transposing the data with grouping by function. It is equivalent to the Pivot Tables function in Excel. Let's take the example above with the weights of the people.

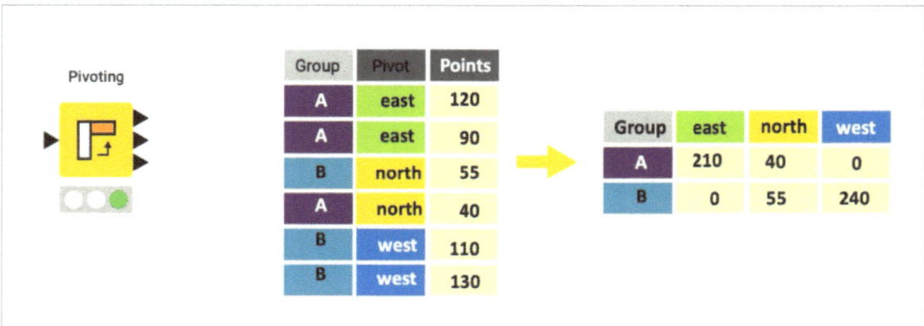

Fig. 2.13 Aggregate data with the Pivoting function

Now you also want to report summary statistics for heart rate and amount of fat mass for every person. You could now split the people into different columns and output the summary statistics in each row, or you could display the people in each row and output the different categories in the columns.

3. Combine Data

a) Join

This is one of the most important concepts in data manipulation and data engineering. And one of the concepts that have not been implemented well in spreadsheet software like Excel and can never be implemented properly. And the reason is simple:

Excel is not suitable for displaying the ETL process.

Joining tables in KNIME is self-explanatory. Simply insert the **Joiner** node and select the desired joiner mode and joining columns. The output of the node will be either an inner join, full outer join, right or left join (see next figure).

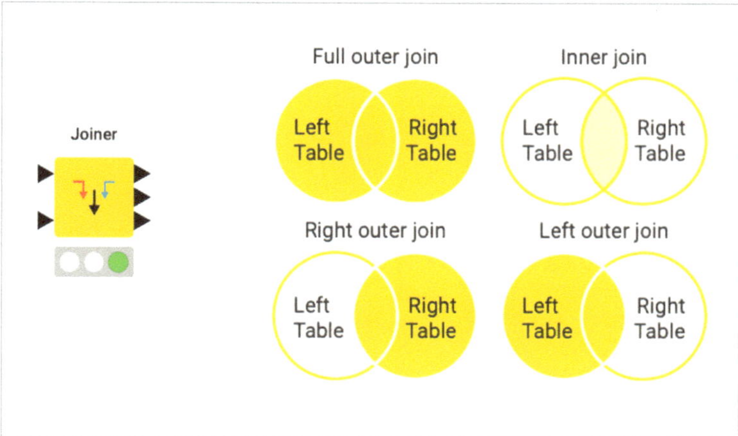

Fig. 2.14 Joining tables

b) Concatenate

Concatenating two tables could not be easier in KNIME. The **Concatenate** node combines two or even more tables into one.

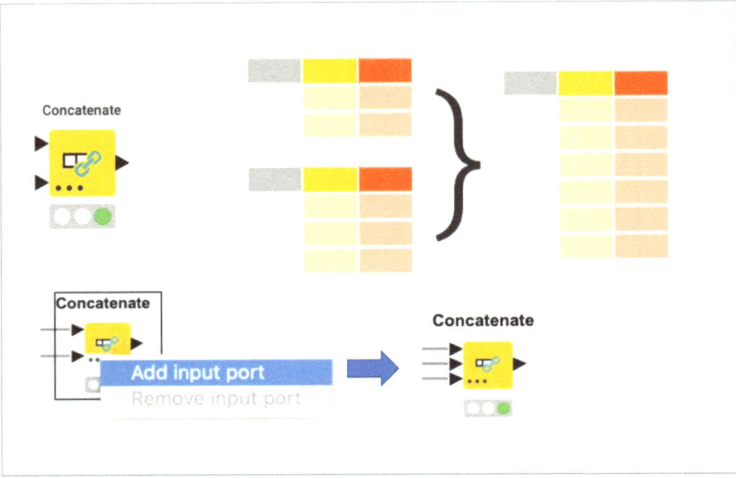

Fig. 2.15 Concatenating tables in KNIME

Learning a visual programming language like KNIME gives you the foundation you need to work efficiently with data.

Not only will you learn to solve your tasks efficiently, but you will also be able to apply the necessary mindset through the visual structure of such a programming language.

Finally, this is the best way to enter the world of data, acquire knowledge quickly and efficiently, and succeed in your daily work.

HERE'S a link to a cheat sheet on data wrangling, along with tips and tricks for KNIME, to help you get a clearer overview:

https://www.knime.com/files/data-wrangling-with-knime.pdf

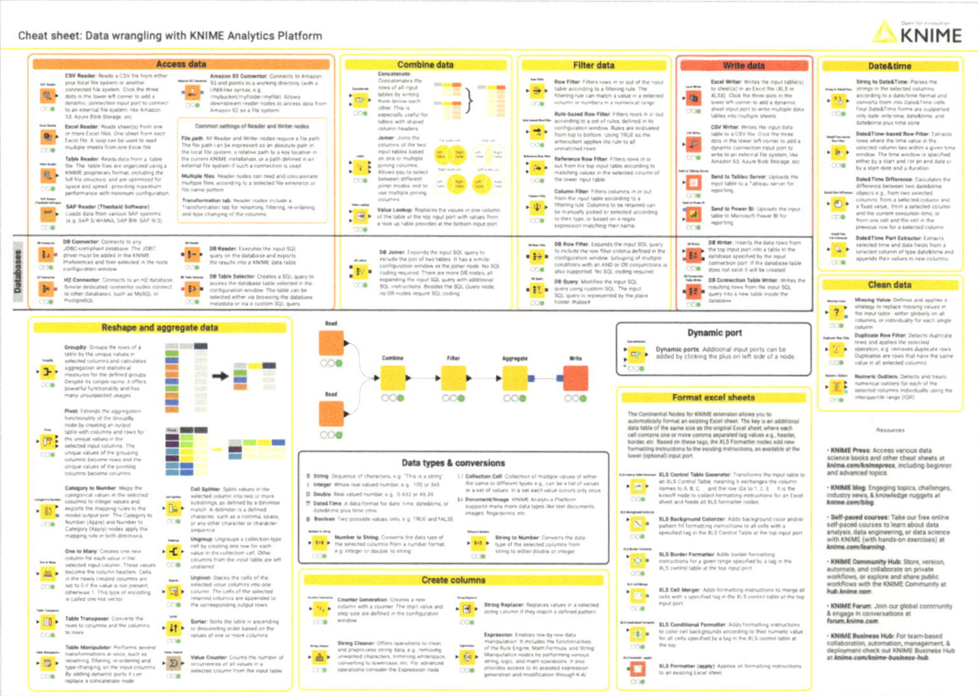

Fig. 2.16 KNIME Cheat Sheet - Data Wrangling

3

BUILDING YOUR OWN DATA SCIENCE INFRASTRUCTURE

Choosing the right software and OS

You will most likely already have a Windows laptop or a Macbook or work with a desktop PC. Some of you will even work with Linux.

First: with the computing power of today's systems, a lot can already be done in the field of data science. But depending on the operating system and system components, such as RAM and CPU power, there are always limitations.

So, let's define the requirements based on the necessary software packages and then decide which operating system is best suited to our needs. In a second step, we install the relevant software packages and check the hardware system requirements.

In order to build our productive data science infrastructure, we need the following packages:

1. **The right data blending and ETL tool**
2. **A user-friendly Python framework**
3. **Database for storage**
4. **A good visualization tool**

For the more advanced data scientist, there is also the following point to consider: **Deep learning capabilities**.

However, it is not a basic prerequisite for running the example exercises in this book. For most data engineers and data analysts, the requirements listed above are always sufficient.

Recent developments in the field of **Generative Artificial Intelligence (GenAI)** have demonstrated that this element should also be considered part of a data science infrastructure. **KNIME** offers a dedicated implementation solution for this as well.

Let's now take a closer look at these packages and see how they fit together in our data science infrastructure.

1.) The right data blending and ETL tool

As I have already explained in the previous chapters, the best tool for data blending and ETL is, in my opinion, KNIME.

There are installation packages of **KNIME** for all three operating systems Windows, macOS and Linux here: https://www.knime.com/downloads

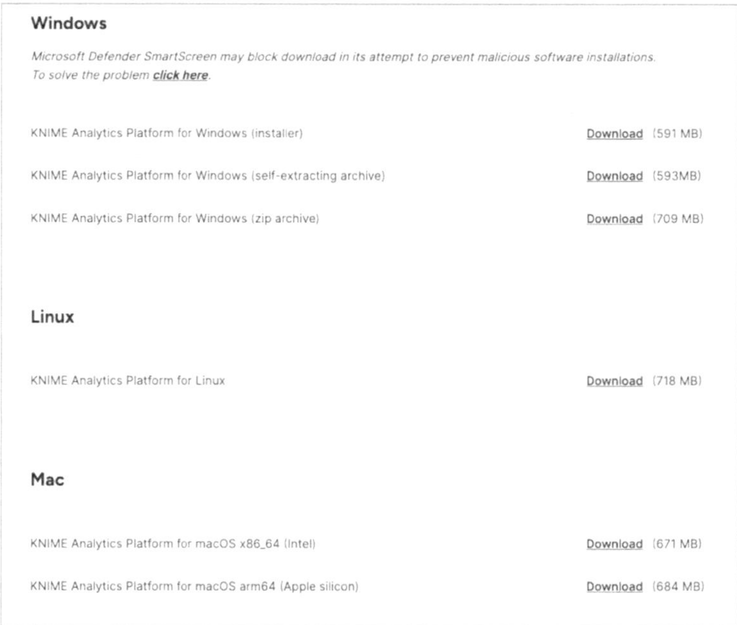

Fig. 3.1 KNIME downloads for Win, macOS and Linux

There are different download options for Windows and, in addition to the Linux version, also for Intel Macs and Silicon Macs.

So, as far as the operating system is concerned, you are free to choose with KNIME.

In this book, we will cover **KNIME 5.5.1**, which is the current version at the time of publication of this book.

Available Operating Systems (KNIME):

- **Windows [yes]**
- **macOS [yes]**
- **Linux [yes]**

2.) A user-friendly Python framework

While **KNIME** provides a comprehensive, no-code solution for covering all aspects of **ETL**, **Python** remains a cornerstone of data science.

Jupyter Notebook's implementation of Python is the first choice for most data scientists. The seamless integration with Python makes it ideal for tasks such as data exploration, analysis and model development. Jupyter's interactive environment allows for easy coding, documentation and visualization - all in one place.

Jupyter can be installed effortlessly through the **Anaconda** framework, which simplifies the process across all operating systems and comes with Python preinstalled.

While Jupyter Notebook is powerful for these tasks, **KNIME** is often better suited for managing more complex **ETL** workflows. Its visual interface is tailored to efficiently handle all stages of ETL, making it the preferred tool when dealing with large-scale data integration tasks.

By integrating KNIME's intuitive ETL features with Python's advanced data manipulation and machine learning libraries, we can build robust, scalable data science workflows that leverage the strengths of both platforms.

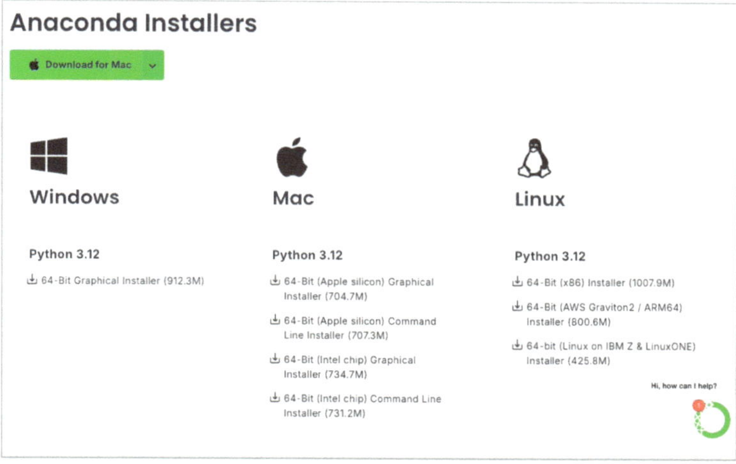

Fig. 3.2 Anaconda downloads for Win, macOS and Linux

Here you will find the download files for **Anaconda**:

https://www.anaconda.com/download/success

Available Operating Systems (Anaconda):

- **Windows [yes]**
- **macOS [yes]**
- **Linux [yes]**

With Anaconda, you also have a free choice of operating system.

3.) Database for storage

To get things easy, we will start with **SQLite** as database-solution. It's not really a sophisticated database like Oracle, MySQL or Teradata, but you can use most SQL commands with it and in combination with KNIME it works very well. In my opinion SQLite is completely underrated.

If KNIME is already installed, there's no need to install any additional SQLite packages.

Otherwise, installation packages for Windows, macOS, and Linux are available here:

https://www.sqlite.org/download.html

Available Operating Systems (SQLite):

- **Windows [yes]**
- **macOS [yes]**
- **Linux [yes]**

4.) A good visualization tool

You won't believe how difficult it is to find a visualization tool that is available for free and offers all the features you need.

Even if you could create your reports with KNIME alone, as we will see in chapter 5, the use of more sophisticated visualization software will be necessary in everyday work with many users.

Tableau Public is my first choice as it includes many elements of the paid version and is available for both Windows and macOS.

Sadly, Linux misses out here. Although many data science tools were originally programmed especially for Linux systems, there are still no good visualization tools that are used at an operational level.

To use the public version of Tableau, you need to know some workarounds to be able to use it in production mode. But it is still the best choice now.

As already mentioned, the installation packages are only available for Windows and macOS. To download Tableau Public, you need to register here:

https://public.tableau.com/app/discover

Available Operating Systems (Tableau Public):

- **Windows [yes]**
- **macOS [yes]**
- **Linux [no]**

All three operating systems are suitable for productive use in data science and data engineering. But if visualization and reporting are also essential, then we are best off with either Windows or macOS.

Choosing the right hardware

We can choose between a ready-made system, which usually comes with a Mac or Windows laptop, or for the more tech-versed of you, build a custom rig. As already mentioned, ready-made systems are already sufficient to handle many data science tasks today

However, if you are dealing with computationally intensive tasks and want to work with a lot of data or use deep learning algorithms, then it pays to know the system components of a computer.

> Just as a skilled truck driver understands the importance of maintenance, a data scientist should be familiar with their hardware.

So, let's go through the individual components.

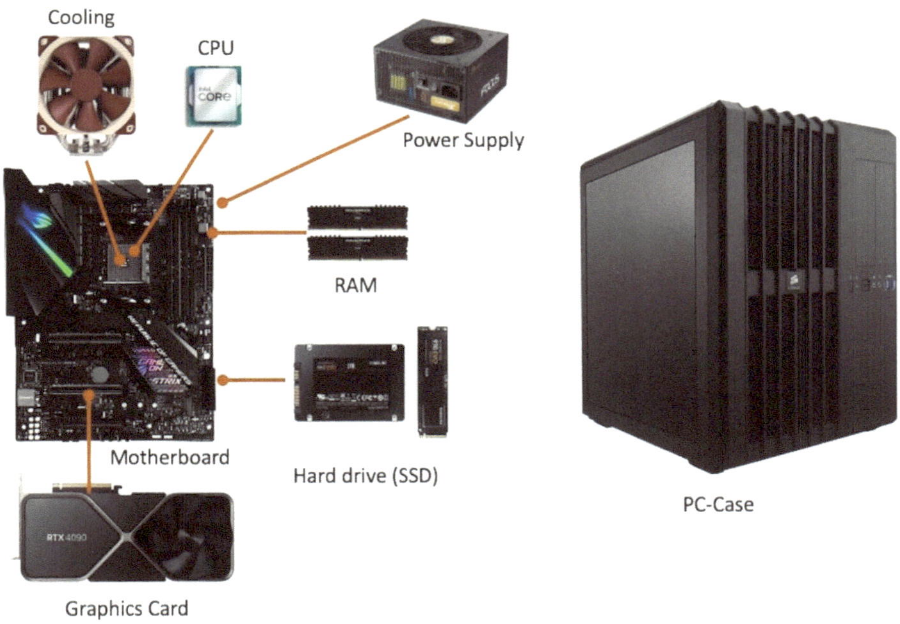

Fig. 3.3 The basic components of a PC

A PC, be it a Mac or Windows desktop/laptop, consists of the following main components:

1. CPU
2. RAM
3. Hard drive
4. GPU (Graphics card)
5. Motherboard
6. PC-Case
7. Cooling
8. PSU (Power supply)

1.) CPU

When working with gigabyte-sized data and performing numerous queries, a powerful **multi-core CPU** can significantly enhance performance.

Many data engineering workflows, such as data processing, ETL pipelines, and distributed computing, can benefit from parallel processing, which utilizes multiple cores. This allows for faster handling of large datasets and more efficient execution of complex operations.

Single-core performance still matters for specific tasks, but for heavy, multi-threaded workloads, multi-core capabilities will make a noticeable difference.

With more cores and threads, your system can distribute data loading tasks across multiple execution units, reducing bottlenecks and improving overall throughput.

In summary, if your workload involves frequent data queries and large datasets, investing in a high-core-count CPU ensures smoother and faster data handling, ultimately optimizing model training and inference times.

The image shows a top 5 **Geekbench** comparison of multi-core results for Intel and AMD processors (left) and Mac processors (right).

Single Core | Multi-Core | | Single Core | Multi-Core | OpenCL | Metal

Processor	Score	Mac	Score
Intel Core i9-13900KS 3.2 GHz (24 cores)	21692	MacBook Pro (16-inch, 2024) Apple M4 Max @ 4.5 GHz (16 CPU cores, 40 GPU cores)	25669
AMD EPYC 9684X 2.6 GHz (96 cores)	21442	MacBook Pro (14-inch, 2024) Apple M4 Max @ 4.5 GHz (16 CPU cores, 40 GPU cores)	25587
AMD EPYC 9374F 3.8 GHz (32 cores)	21440	Mac Studio (2023) Apple M2 Ultra @ 3.7 GHz (24 CPU cores, 60 GPU cores)	21363
Intel Xeon Platinum 8462Y+ 2.8 GHz (32 cores)	20762	Mac Studio (2023) Apple M2 Ultra @ 3.7 GHz (24 CPU cores, 76 GPU cores)	21363
Intel Core i9-14900KF 3.2 GHz (24 cores)	20687	Mac Pro (2023) Apple M2 Ultra @ 3.7 GHz (24 CPU cores, 60 GPU cores)	21294

Fig. 3.4 Geekbench for Multi-Core - Left Intel/AMD, right Mac M's

It seems that the actual Macbook Pro 2024, despite its relatively high price, is the best choice. You do not have to choose the best processor, as this is also related to costs. But such tables should help you make the right choice when buying.

The CPU alone is not enough. We also need to consider other criteria.

2.) RAM

Choosing the right amount of RAM is crucial for data science and data engineering tasks. While factors like speed and latency matter, the most important aspect is capacity - more RAM generally leads to better performance.

For large datasets, such as images, log files, or big structured data, having enough RAM to fit the entire dataset in memory can drastically improve processing speed. Insufficient RAM forces reliance on slower disk-based operations, creating performance bottlenecks.

Capacity: At least **16GB** is recommended for moderate workloads, while **32GB+** is ideal for handling large datasets.

On a Mac, especially with Apple's M-series chips, 16GB of RAM often feels more powerful compared to 16GB on a traditional Windows machine. This is mainly due to the Unified Memory Architecture in Macs, where CPU, GPU, and Neural Engine share the same memory pool. This seamless memory sharing allows for faster data access and lower latency, which can significantly enhance performance in data science tasks, particularly with large datasets or when running multiple processes.

In contrast, on a Windows PC, RAM is typically split between the CPU and GPU, which can lead to inefficiencies if you run out of system RAM and need to swap to disk. This makes having more RAM critical to avoid slowdowns during data-intensive operations.

In summary, while 32GB is beneficial for both platforms, the way memory is utilized in Macs often makes it feel more efficient, allowing you to push larger datasets or more complex models without hitting performance bottlenecks.

This means that 16 GB can usually be sufficient for a Mac in the daily work environment.

In short, investing in higher RAM capacity ensures smooth data processing, reducing delays and improving efficiency in machine learning, analytics, and ETL workflows.

Bear this in mind when buying a laptop, as not every laptop allows you to upgrade the RAM.

3.) Hard drive

For data science and data engineering tasks, storage is just as crucial as RAM - more capacity and speed are key. To optimize data loading, **NVMe SSDs** are now the best option. These drives offer dramatically faster speeds compared to traditional SATA SSDs, reducing loading times and improving overall performance.

I recommend installing or using a **500GB SSD** for the OS and software, and a **1-2TB NVMe SSD** for data storage to ensure the fastest performance in data-intensive workflows.

When RAM is full, the system uses **virtual memory** (disk space) to compensate, but this process is much slower. Therefore, having enough RAM and fast SSD storage ensures that large datasets and heavy computations are handled efficiently without significant slowdowns from relying on disk memory.

4.) GPU (Graphics Card)

In recent years, the importance of **GPUs** in deep learning and data science has grown dramatically. Modern deep learning models have become more complex, requiring **massive parallel computation**, which GPUs handle far more efficiently than CPUs.

Tasks like **training neural networks and processing vast datasets** rely heavily on GPU acceleration, making them a key component of any high-performance data science PC.

NVIDIA remains the industry leader for deep learning due to **CUDA** and **Tensor Cores**, which accelerate key matrix calculations in frameworks like **TensorFlow, PyTorch,** and **JAX**.

The latest **RTX 40-series (4070, 4080, 4090)** offer significant improvements in speed and VRAM capacity, making them ideal for training **state-of-the-art** (SOTA) deep learning models.

Apple's M-series chips (M1, M2, M3, and M4) integrate **Unified Memory** and a **Neural Engine**, optimizing ML workflows with Metal Performance Shaders and **Core ML**.

While they lack native CUDA support, frameworks like **TensorFlow-Metal** allow macOS users to train models efficiently, especially for research and prototyping.

For a **high-performance data science PC**, **NVIDIA GPUs** remain the best choice for flexibility and scalability. However, **Apple's M-series** provides a competitive alternative for those working within the macOS ecosystem.

The previous components apply to both laptops and desktop computers. However, if you want to build your own PC, the following components, which are already predefined for laptops, must be chosen properly.

5.) Motherboard

If you want to build your own machine you should make sure that the motherboard is compatible with your CPU and RAM. It is always a good choice to buy the motherboard together with the CPU in one package.

When choosing a motherboard make sure it has enough PCIe slots for the numbers of GPUs you want. The rule here is one GPU will take up space for 2 PCIe slots.

Another point is the form factor. I would definitely choose a classic ATX motherboard here, since our goal is not to build a small-factor PC, but a high-performance data science solution.

6.) PC-Case

Over the past few years, I've built several PCs myself. However, it's important to consider these key points:

The case should offer enough space for all components, be easy to assemble, and provide good airflow. Always keep an eye on the temperature, as performing complex data tasks or calculations can cause the machine to heat up significantly over time.

Fig. 3.5 One of my custom PC builds of the last years

The PC shown in the image is built using the **Corsair Carbide Series Air** case.

7.) Cooling

A strong cooler is very important for keeping a system's temperature low. A water-cooling setup offers high performance and reduces noise, but not always.

I have tried different setups in the past and have to say that even a good air cooler can be quiet. And most certainly it usually takes less space and is also easier to install. Here comes the advantage of an AMD Ryzen CPU. It heats up less quickly than an Intel CPU.

8.) PSU (Power supply)

We now have almost all our components. The next question is: How much power will our system need?

There are various PSU calculators for calculating the required power:

https://www.bequiet.com/en/psucalculator

For my system, for example, a 360 W power supply unit would have been sufficient at the time. However, to ensure that I have enough power if I add a second graphics card in the future, I opted for a PSU that offers 750 W in the end.

Here it is simply important to provide the system with sufficient power so that all components run smoothly.

To create your own system, go to **PC Part Picker**:

https://pcpartpicker.com/

The advantage of a self-built PC is the cost and the possible hardware extensions. With \$1,500-\$3,000 you can build a very powerful machine where a ready-made system would be more expensive.

A cloud service solution can also become very expensive over time, but it can of course be scaled even better.

Finally, it is important to consider the needs and the corresponding financial resources so that an appropriate solution can be implemented.

Installation of the software

If you have chosen a laptop, you do not need to install an operating system. For those who want to build their own system, we now install Windows.

1.) Windows OS (installation)

After assembling the whole system, we need to install an operating system OS. In our example, we will set up a Windows system.

We could also set up an Intel Mac system, a so-called **Hackintosh**, but the hurdles would be higher, and hardware compatibility would be much more complicated. Additionally, every macOS update would require corresponding tweaks. Moreover, Apple is focusing on its own M-series Silicon chips in the future, gradually reducing support for Intel Macs.

The first step is to download Windows and **create an installation media**. We will copy the installation files on an USB-stick.

The following steps are taken from Windows Support site. Search the internet for: „Create installation media for Windows".

1. Go to the Download Windows 11 site here: https://www.microsoft.com/en-us/software-download/windows11
2. Under Create Windows 11 Installation Media, select Download Now. The **MediaCreationTool.exe** tool is downloaded.
3. Run **MediaCreationTool.exe**. The media creation tool walks through creating installation media.

The following items are required to create the installation media:

- A PC with internet connection
- A blank USB flash drive with at least 8 GB of space.
- A Windows 11 product key.

2.) GPU NVIDIA and CUDA-Drivers (installation)

To get the best out of your NVIDIA graphics card, whether on a Windows laptop or desktop, you need the appropriated **NVIDIA drivers**. In addition to the normal GPU drivers, the **Cuda toolkit** must also be installed.

The **CUDA Toolkit** is necessary in **Data Science** when you need to leverage **GPU acceleration** for computationally intensive tasks. It allows data scientists to use **NVIDIA GPUs** to accelerate machine learning, deep learning, and large-scale data processing.

While KNIME itself does not natively rely on CUDA, it supports **TensorFlow and Keras**, which can use CUDA to run on GPUs. You can configure KNIME nodes to use a GPU-accelerated TensorFlow installation to train e.g. deep learning models.

TensorFlow is an open-source machine learning framework developed by Google, designed for building and deploying deep learning models efficiently. It supports both **CPU and GPU acceleration** using CUDA for high-performance computations.

Keras is a high-level deep learning API running on top of TensorFlow, providing an easy-to-use interface for building neural networks with minimal code. It simplifies model creation, training, and evaluation while still leveraging TensorFlow's powerful backend

---

Apple's M-series lack native CUDA support. Here you must switch to frameworks like **TensorFlow-Metal** to train deep learning models efficiently.

LET'S go back to the beginning of chapter 3.1 and download and install the discussed software for our data science infrastructure.

3.) Jupyter Notebook by Anaconda (installation)

Jupyter can be easily installed using the Anaconda framework, which streamlines the setup on all operating systems and includes Python by default. Choose the appropriate installer for your system here:

https://www.anaconda.com/download/success

When the installation is complete, you can start Jupyter Notebook from the corresponding tile (see the red arrow in the next picture)

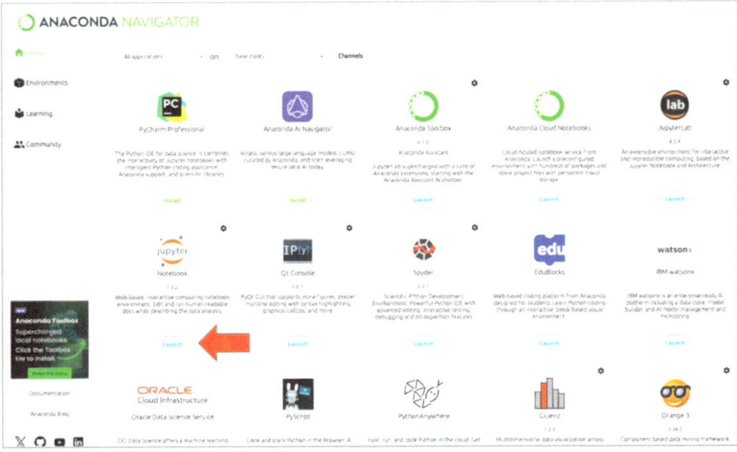

Fig. 3.6 Starting Jupyter Notebook from Anaconda

You can now use Jupyter from the following address in the browser of your local machine: http://localhost:8888/tree

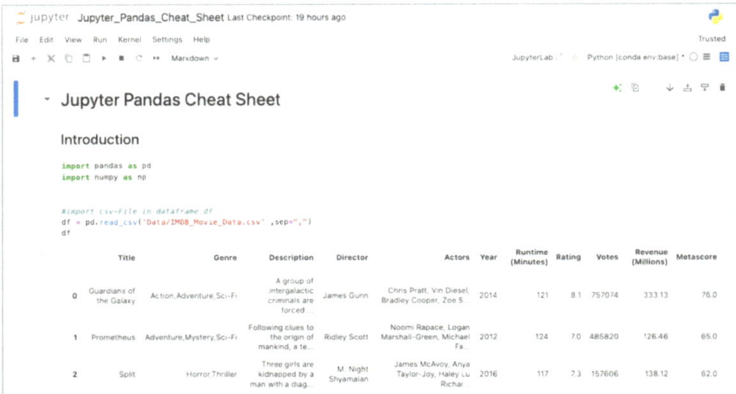

Fig. 3.7 Jupyter Notebook in the browser

4.) KNIME (installation)

KNIME is at the heart of our data science infrastructure, as it will orchestrate everything from data blending to machine learning and deep learning to preparation for visualization.

Download your appropriate installer here:

https://www.knime.com/downloads

Before you start the installation, there are two points to consider:

1. Specify memory settings for KNIME

When you start KNIME, a window asks for the location of your workspace. This workspace is by default a folder on your computer where all your KNIME workflows are saved.

Depending on how much RAM is available on your system, I would reserve 10 GB RAM for the system and the rest for KNIME. With 32 GB of RAM, 22 GB would then be available for KNIME.

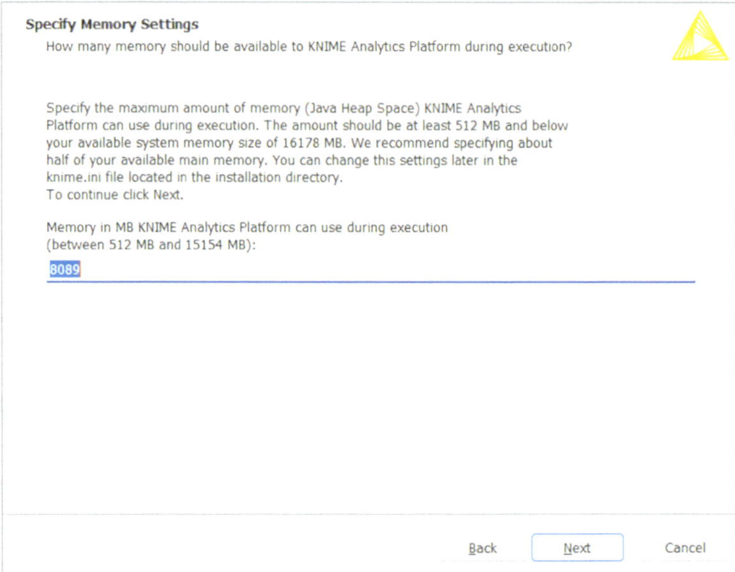

Fig. 3.8 Specify memory settings in KNIME

You can change the memory settings in the knime.ini file at any time. But be careful when doing so!

The knime.ini file can be edited with a text editor and is located here in Windows:

C:\Program Files\KNIME\knime.ini

On macOS go to the Applications folder select the KNIME app and **Show Package Contents** by clicking the right mouse button.

You should now see this:

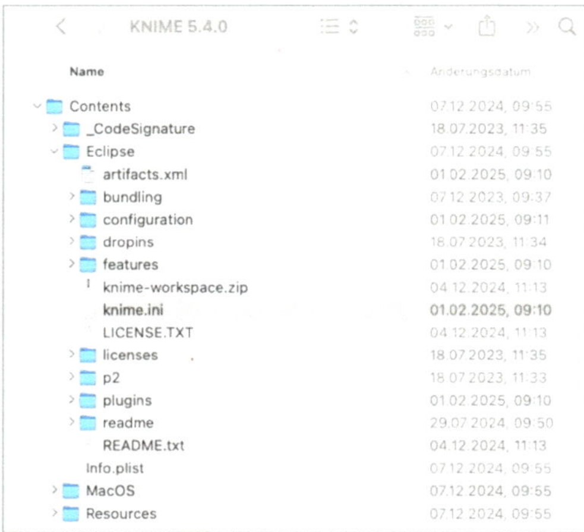

Fig. 3.9 Edit knime.ini file on macOS

Open the file and search for -Xmx. If you want to reserve 8 GB of RAM for KNIME, write -Xmx8G; to reserve 24 GB, write -Xmx24G.

2. Specify the Workspace for KNIME

When you start KNIME, a window asks for the location of your workspace. This workspace is by default a folder on your computer where all your KNIME workflows are saved.

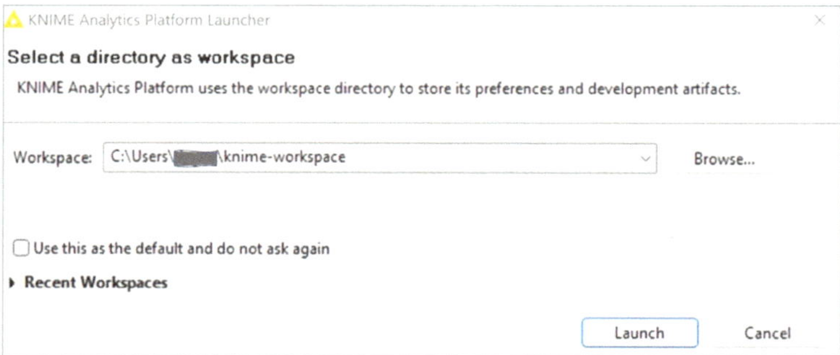

Fig. 3.10 Choosing the KNIME workspace

If you want to choose a folder in your cloud service such as **Onedrive**, Google Drive etc. for your workspace, then be warned! I've tested them all so far and I have to say, without making any commercials, that only Onedrive is the best for this task.

The reason for this is that all other cloud services have problems synchronizing the KNIME files. This is because the KNIME workflows are made up of many files. And every manipulation of a knime workflow causes synchronization.

Therefore, either use the default workspace on your own machine or choose Onedrive.

If you want to change the workspace later, you can do this in KNIME via menu

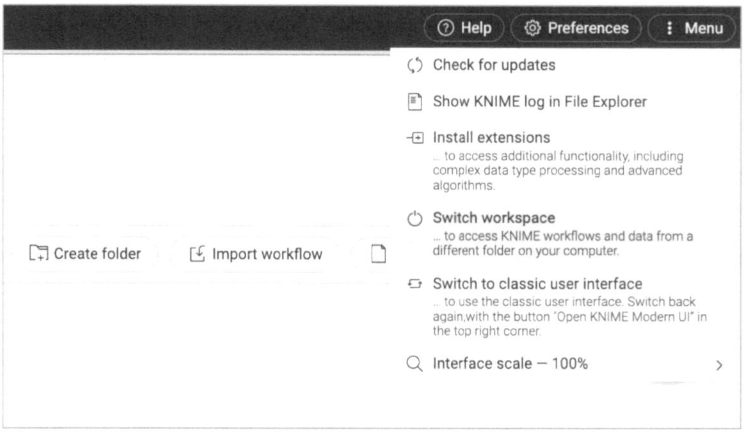

Fig. 3.11 Changing workspace in KNIME

Another option would be to work directly on the **KNIME Community Hub**:

https://hub.knime.com/

It is definitely a good option to familiarize yourself with the KNIME Community Hub and register for free. This way, you can not only download all the workflows and solutions of other users but also save your own workflows in the KNIME Cloud and make them available to other users or keep your work private just for yourself.

There are many good tutorials and introductory courses on KNIME. In the next chapter, we will therefore only go into the basic operation principles. Based on this understanding, using the software should be mostly intuitive. However, I will also provide the relevant learning resources and links at the end of the chapter.

5.) SQLite (installation)

Now comes an easy part: If you already have KNIME installed, then nothing else needs to be installed. You can already create, read and write your own SQLite databases.

SQLite is a relational database management system (RDBMS) contained in a C library. In contrast to many other database management systems, SQLite is not a client–server database engine. Rather, it is embedded into the end program.

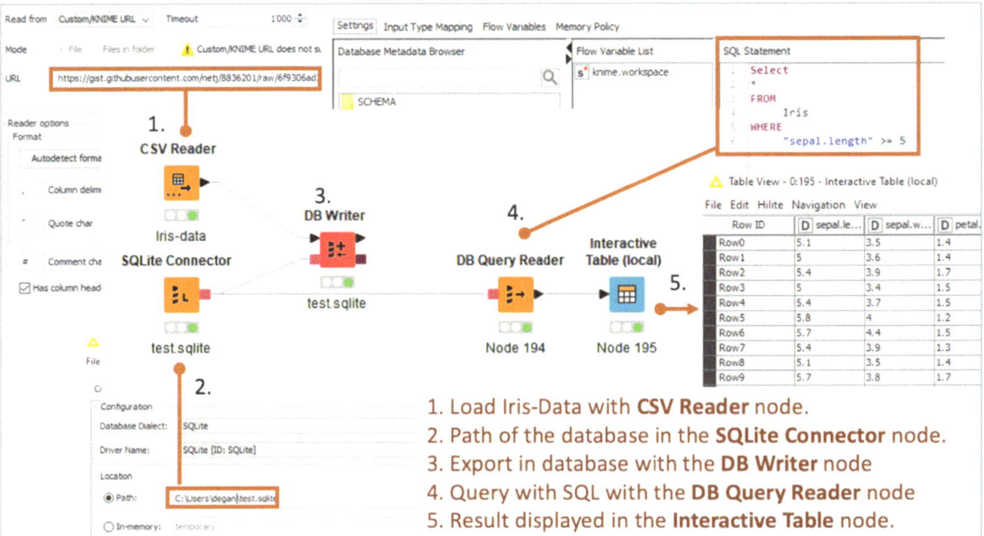

Fig. 3.12 Creating and querying a SQLite database with KNIME

6.) Tableau Public (installation)

To get Tableau Public, you need to sign up for a free profile. But it's definitely worth it, because you get an online space to share your Tableau Dashboards anywhere on the web.

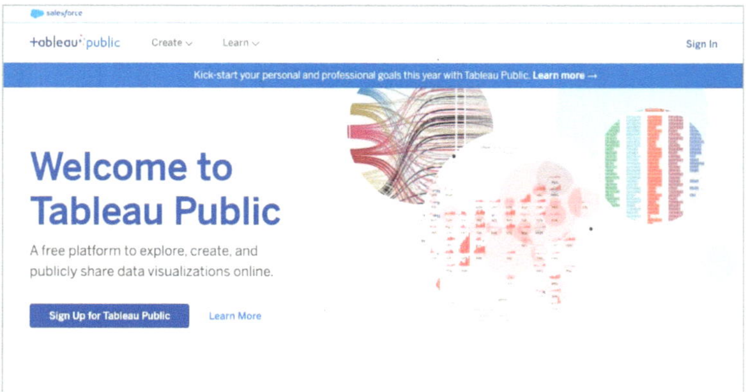

Fig. 3.13 Sign up at Tableau Public

https://www.tableau.com/products/public/download

After downloading and installing Tableau Public, you can also sign in to the Tableau Public site with the same account, where you can upload your Tableau boards and share them with other users.

https://public.tableau.com/app/discover

This is not an introductory book on Tableau. For tutorials and beginner courses, I will have to refer you to the corresponding resources.

Now you should be ready to get into data science, equipped with a solid infrastructure that includes both the right hardware and essential software tools.

With a well-equipped PC or laptop that has sufficient computing power, memory and storage space, you should be able to perform complex data operations efficiently.

Your software suite, consisting of KNIME for ETL and workflow automation, Anaconda for Python and Tableau for data visualization, provides a solid foundation for data analysis, machine learning and business intelligence.

4

THE BEST KEPT SECRET IN DATA SCIENCE

KNIME is open source

More and more often, I'm getting questions from Business Analysts, BI Specialists, and Data Engineers such as:

> "Why KNIME? Can you show me a demo? And how do you use it in your company?"

Depending on their level of knowledge, they also ask me:

> „I've heard there's a free, open-source version available. But the premium version isn't free, is it?"

Some of them are experienced data engineers and often use well-known tools such as SAS, Alteryx, and Python.

> "I can do this and that in SPSS, SAS, Alteryx, Python,... can you do the same with KNIME?"

And of course, coders always want to code:

> "I have heard that it is a No-Code tool. But why don't you code?"

All these people have heard or seen that we have been using KNIME successfully in our company for over a decade.

Some of those who have evaluated the software say:

> "It's a no-code tool that you can use to create data pipelines. Our XYZ tool can do that too!".

In the past, it was very difficult to find interested data engineers or business analysts for KNIME. They were satisfied with their (expensive) tools. Today, they come to me on their own.

But why this sudden change of heart?

If you search for the keyword KNIME on Google Trends, you'll see that searches have risen steadily since July 2006, when the first public version was released.

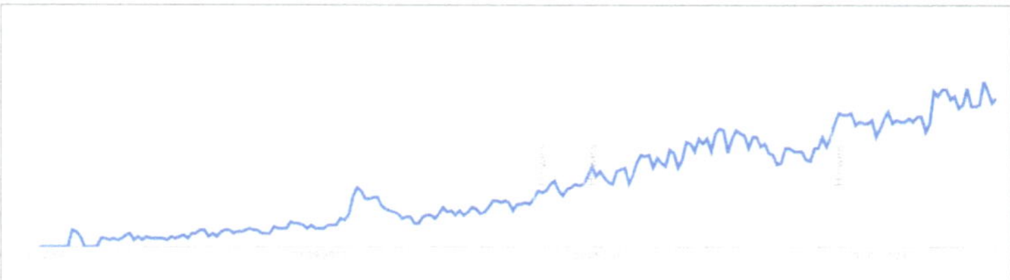

Fig. 4.1 Google trends for the search "KNIME" since 2006

Two reasons seem to be gaining in importance:

1.) Companies start saving on licensing costs as well

Not so long ago, if you worked for a large company, it was no big deal to renew the high license costs for data tools like SAS or IBM Modeler.

Nowadays, it's "We're not paying anymore. Find a cheaper tool!"

2.) Collaboration between Business Analysts, Developers and Data Scientists

In the past, business analysts only worked with Excel. Today, more and more of them are realizing that they can work more efficiently with a low-code or no-code tool.

On the other hand, developers only want to code. Collaboration on this basis is very difficult. Misunderstandings and the repetition of certain tasks are inevitable.

The solution would be a less expensive or open-source tool that offers a programming language that allows both business analysts and developers to work together on the same platform and according to the same principles. And for us, that solution so far has been **KNIME**.

KNIME covers all these aspects:

- It is and will remain **open source**, as this is the basis of the KNIME philosophy
- Provides a **Low-Code** platform suitable for business analysts as well as developers, data engineers and data scientists
- It is **cross-platform software**, with versions available for Windows as well as for macOS and Linux.

KNIME and Openness

KNIME is built on a foundation of *openness* and community collaboration. Its core philosophy is to offer a comprehensive open-source platform that meets the diverse needs of users, while continuously growing through both internal development and valuable contributions from the community.

Unlike other open-source products, KNIME is not a cut-down version and there are no artificial limitations on execution environment or data size.

If you have enough local or cloud-based space and compute power, you can run projects with billions of rows, as many KNIME users currently do.

The second point covers the Low-Code approach. Because as we have already learned:

The best representation of an ETL pipeline is a visual workflow.

The visual environment provides just the right amount of abstraction to build and share your work. Yes, because you will always be working with others and therefore need to be able to document and share your work.

Nowadays no data scientist or data engineer works alone anymore. We are all part of teams, and we all need to communicate together. Discussion of the tasks, best practices, documentation are all necessary tasks in the daily work.

Once KNIME has been installed, locate your instance of KNIME from the appropriate folder, desktop link, application, or Start menu link, and start it.

Before we get started with a concrete example, we need to familiarize ourselves with the elementary concepts in KNIME.

The KNIME Graphics User Interface (GUI)

1.) The Workspace

When the start screen appears, a window will ask for the location of your workspace. As we saw in Chapter 3 when installing KNIME, this workspace is a folder on your computer or on a cloud server where all your work is saved.

You can organize workflows into folders, import/export workflows, and manage different workspace locations for different projects.

2.) The Workbench and the Explorer

The Workbench is the place where you will build your workflows. You will also find all the necessary resources here.

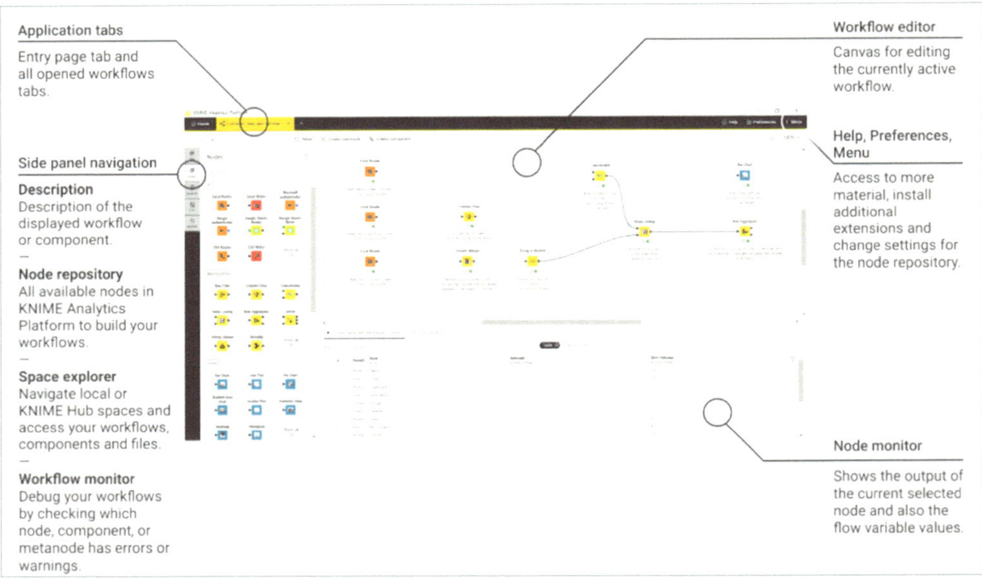

Fig. 4.2 The KNIME Workbench

The Workflow Editor is what you'll be using to build your workflows. Workflows are made up of individual tasks, which we refer to as "nodes".

They perform all kinds of operations, for example reading or writing files, transforming data, training models, creating visualizations etc.

You build your workflow by dragging nodes from the Node Repository (left side of the image above) to the Workflow Editor, then connecting, configuring, and executing them.

3.) Nodes and Workflows

In KNIME, individual tasks are represented by nodes. They are the smallest possible unit in KNIME and have been created to perform all sorts of tasks, including reading/writing files, transforming data, training models, creating visualizations, and so on.

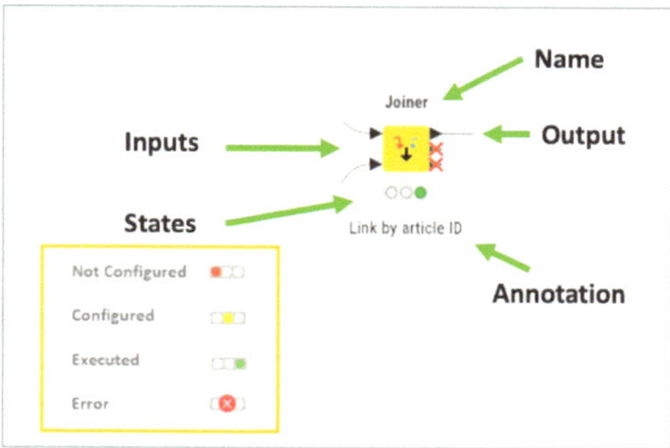

Fig. 4.3 The **Joiner** node performs tasks on data

A sequence of nodes creates a workflow. A workflow - as a sequence of nodes - is the graphic equivalent to a script or a series of instructions.

For example, the following workflow reads an adult demographic data file and builds a decision tree model to predict the income group.

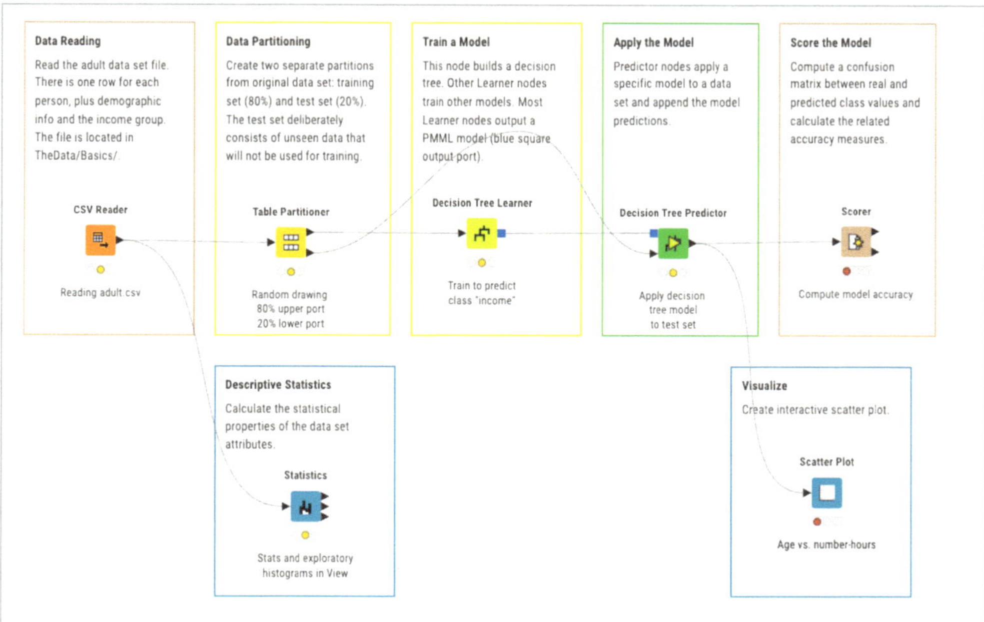

Fig. 4.4 Workflow for predicting the income based on demographic factors

4.) The Node Repository

You will find **Node Repository** in your KNIME workbench in the bottom left-hand corner. It contains the nodes that can be used in your workflow.

The nodes are organized in categories. Each category represents a specific functionality in data analytics.

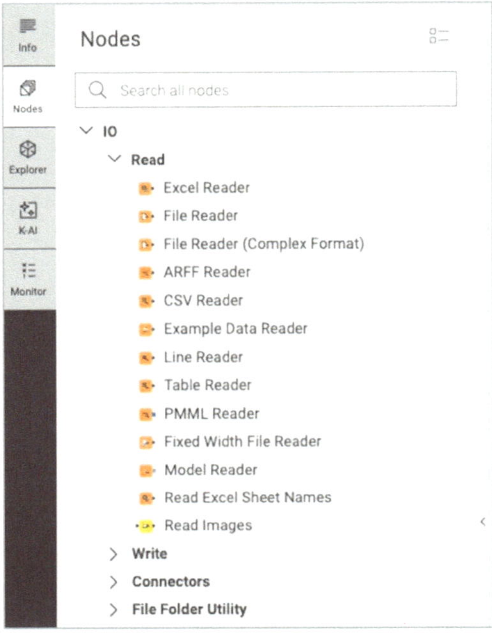

Fig. 4.5 The Node Repository — the "IO > Read" subcategory

IO for example, contains the nodes you need to access data, for file reading and writing, using a number of file formats, such as csv, excel, pmml, images, tables and more.

The **Manipulation** category contains nodes for filtering, aggregating, and transforming data tables. For example for column operations we have a number of column filters, conversions, joining, splitting, and a number of transformation nodes.

Just to quote one of the most commonly used: the **Joiner** node.

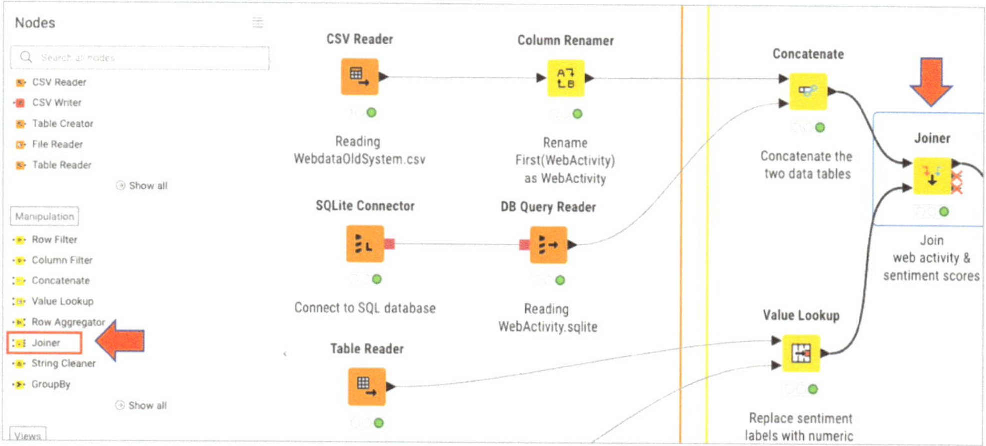

Fig. 4.6 Joining different data sources with the **Joiner** node

You can see in the image how the **Joiner** node in KNIME is used to combine several datasets from multiple sources - including CSV files and an SQLite database - based on a common key.

The workflow in the central pane shows data being read and then processed through several nodes, such as **Column Renamer**, **DB Query Reader**, and **Value Lookup**. Specifically highlighted on the right is the Joiner node, which is used to join web activity data with sentiment scores.

5.) KNIME Extensions

At its core, KNIME provides an intuitive visual workflow editor that enables users to manipulate data, build predictive models, and automate complex processes without extensive programming knowledge.

But what if your specific needs extend beyond the core functionalities? What if you require specialized tools for text analytics, cheminformatics, connecting to a niche database, or even harnessing the power of cutting-edge Large Language Models (LLMs)?

This is where the true power and flexibility of KNIME shines through: **KNIME Extensions**.

Think of KNIME Extensions as modular add-ons, carefully crafted to expand the capabilities of the platform. They are like specialized toolboxes; each packed with nodes designed for a particular domain or task. Whether you're dealing with social media data, genomic sequences, financial time series, or the complexities of natural language processing, there's a good chance an extension exists to streamline your workflow. These extensions, developed by

KNIME itself, community members, or even third-party organizations, seamlessly integrate into KNIME, extending its reach far beyond its initial boundaries.

This includes extensions that bridge the gap between KNIME and the rapidly evolving world of LLMs, enabling you to incorporate these powerful models directly into your data science workflows. Imagine leveraging LLMs for sentiment analysis, text summarization, or even generating synthetic data, all within the familiar KNIME environment.

6.) The KNIME AI Assistant (K-AI)

In addition to the wealth of free resources, you might find it helpful to receive guidance when it comes to approaching and developing your workflows. This is where AI can make a difference.

The KNIME AI Assistant (K-AI) extension becomes an invaluable ally, assisting in node selection and connections rather than in critical decision-making.

To benefit from K-AI, you don't even need to select the node. Just drag a connection from a node's port onto the canvas and prompt K-AI to continue building the workflow from there.

K-AI documents the workflow steps for you, so you can understand what it did and easily double-check them.

K-AI offers two modes:

1. **Q&A Mode**: Users can ask KNIME-related technical or theoretical questions, and K-AI provides answers, helping users better understand how specific nodes work or how to improve their workflows.
2. **Build Mode**: After Build Mode is activated, K-AI builds the workflow for you by adding, connecting, and configuring nodes based on user interactions. Users can build a workflow with a single prompt or ask for suggestions on what to do next. K-AI can also assist with generating embedded Python or R scripts, and more.

KNIME's K-AI companion doesn't just help build from scratch - it can also extend existing workflows. In Q&A mode, it recommends extensions, workflows, and nodes from the KNIME Community Hub, making it easier than ever to discover and reuse existing solutions.

Learning Resources

A GUI-based tool can be learned and applied in less time than a code-based tool, freeing up again precious time and resources for more important investigations. KNIME supports this with a variety of easy-to-access learning resources:

1.) KNIME Self-Paced Courses

This courses are free and allow you to learn from the basics to get into machine learning. Courses are organized by level: L1 basic, L2 advanced, L3 deployment, L4 specialized.

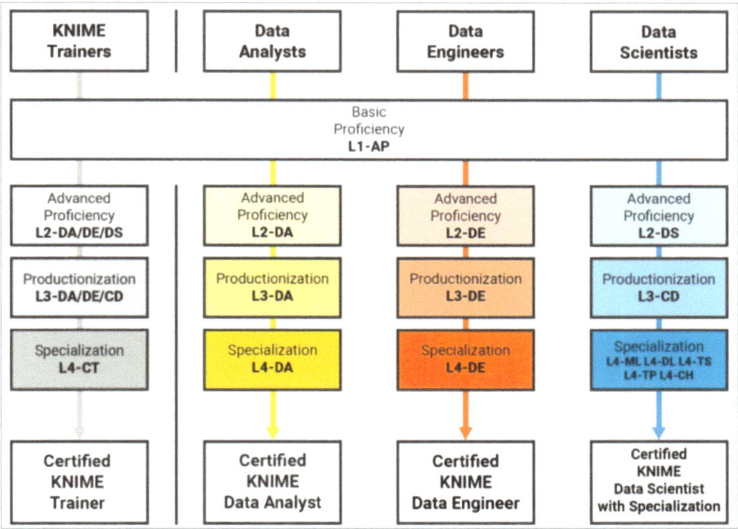

Fig. 4.7 Roadmap of Self-Paced Courses

In each course, go through the lessons with ~5 minutes videos, hands-on exercises, and knowledge-check questions.

2.) KNIME Cheat Sheets

People absorb information in different ways. Some prefer learning through books, others through video playlists or structured courses that follow a clear sequence. But there are also those who have limited time and want quick, direct insights into how things work.

For learners who prefer immediate answers, there is a collection of **cheat sheets** available to help you quickly build your skills with KNIME.

The cheat sheets are organized by learning level, type of data profession, and area of specialization. All are available for free on the **KNIME Press page**.

https://www.knime.com/knimepress

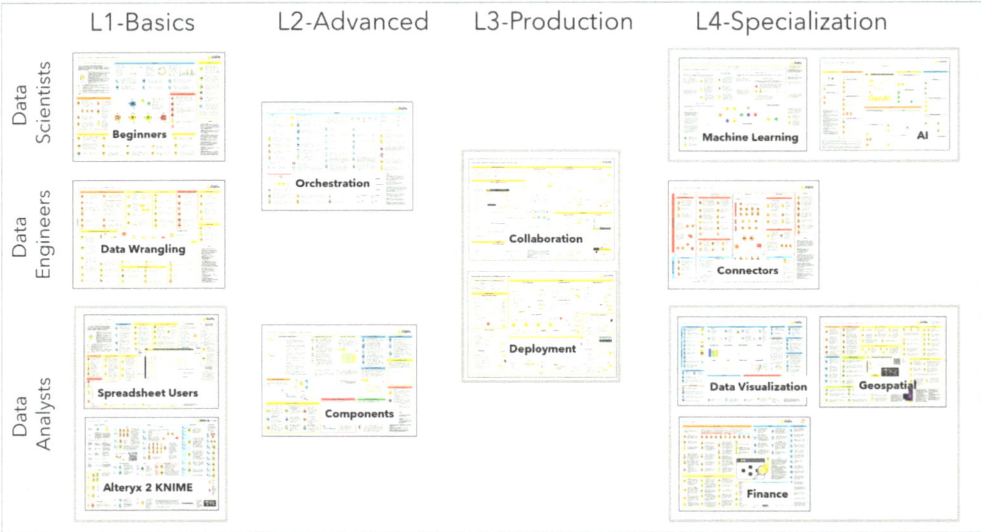

Fig. 4.8 Overview of all KNIME Cheat Sheets

The KNIME cheat sheets support all four levels of learning in the KNIME Learning Center:

- **L1: Basics** – Introductory resources for beginners learning KNIME.
  - **Cheat sheets**: *Beginners, Data Wrangling, Spreadsheet Users, Alteryx 2 KNIME*
- **L2: Advanced** – Intermediate skills like workflow control, automation, and dashboarding.
  - **Cheat sheets**: *Orchestration, Components.*
- **L3: Production** – Best practices for scaling, collaborating, and deploying workflows in KNIME Business Hub.
  - **Cheat sheets**: *Collaboration, Deployment.*
- **L4: Specialization** – Field-specific expertise in data science, engineering, and analytics.
  - **Cheat sheets**: *Machine Learning,* AI, *Connectors, Data Visualization, Geospatial, Finance.*

In addition to learning levels, the cheat sheets are also grouped by data profession to support role-specific learning paths:

- **Data Analysts**: *Spreadsheet Users, Alteryx 2 KNIME, Orchestration, Components, Collaboration, Deployment, Machine Learning, AI, Data Visualization, Geospatial, Finance,*
- **Data Engineers**: *Data Wrangling, Orchestration, Components, Browse and Collaborate, Deployment, Connectors*
- **Data Scientists:** *Beginners, Orchestration, Components, Collaboration, Deployment, Machine Learning, AI*

3.) The KNIME Community Hub

The KNIME Community Hub is the public repository for the KNIME community. Here, you can share your workflows and download workflows created by other KNIME users.

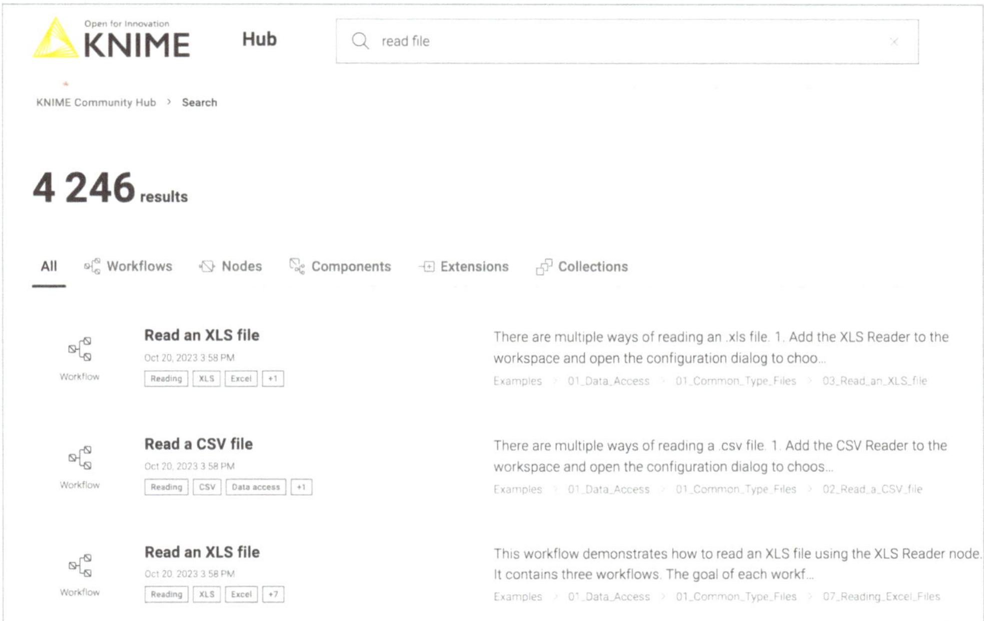

Fig. 4.9 Search the topic "read file" on the KNIME Community Hub

Just type in the keywords and you will get a list of related workflows, components, extensions, and more. It is a great place to start with plenty of examples!

https://hub.knime.com/

For example, just type in the search box "read file" and you will get a list of example workflows illustrating how to read CSV files, table files, excel files, etc.

Once you've identified the workflow you're interested in, click on it to open its details page. From there, you can download it or open it directly in KNIME.

Once in the local workspace, you can start adapting it to your data and your needs. You can just download, reuse, and readapt workflows or pieces of workflows from the KNIME Community Hub to your own problem.

4.) Books about KNIME

The **KNIME Press** offers a diverse collection of resources tailored for individuals aiming to enhance their proficiency with KNIME.

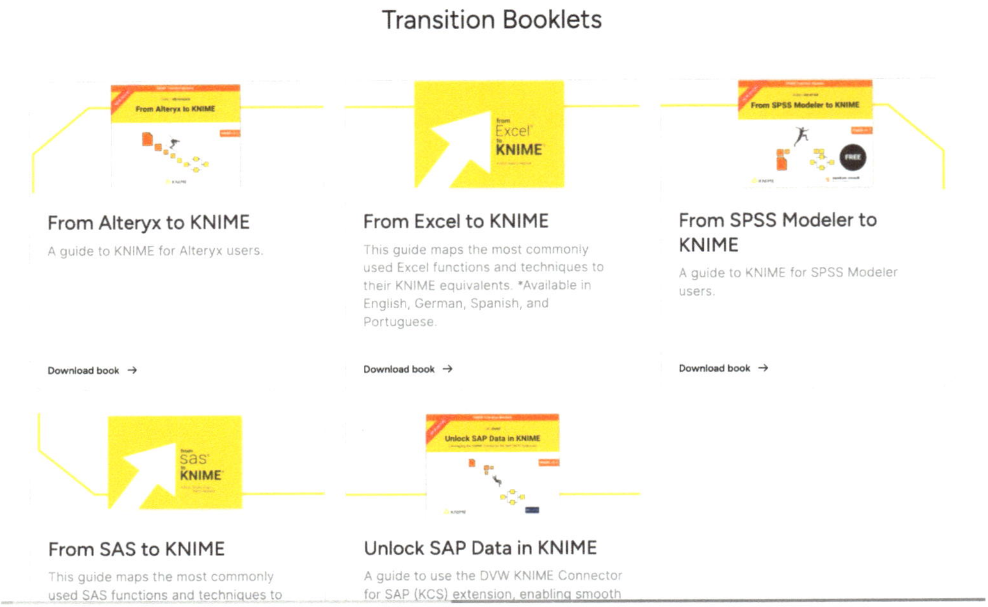

Fig. 4.10 Transition Booklets for users with similar tools

Whether you're a beginner, an experienced user transitioning from other tools, or seeking specialization in areas like text mining, the KNIME Press provides structured learning materials to support your journey:

https://www.knime.com/knimepress

Textbooks: Step-by-step guides such as *KNIME Beginner's Luck* and *KNIME Advanced Luck*, ideal for building foundational and advanced skills in data analytics using KNIME.

Transition Booklets: Free, side-by-side comparisons designed to help users transition smoothly from other platforms like **Excel, SAS, Alteryx, and SPSS** to KNIME.

Use Case Collections: Thematic books like *Will They Blend?, KNIME for Life*

Sciences, and *Practicing Data Science*, showcasing real-world applications and industry-specific workflows.

5.) KNIME TV on YouTube

Be sure to also check out the **KNIME TV Channel** on YouTube. With a wide range of tutorials, webinars, and other resources, this channel is an invaluable for anyone looking to master KNIME. Whether you're a beginner just getting started or an experienced data scientist, the KNIME TV Channel has something for you.

https://www.youtube.com/user/KNIMETV

6.) KNIME on Medium

On Medium, the journal **Low Code for Data Science** regularly publishes successful data science stories, practical tips for getting started with KNIME, insights into data science concepts, and more. Best of all, it features articles written by the community for the community.

Find out how to contribute and share your stories here:

https://medium.com/low-code-for-advanced-data-science

Data Access with KNIME

In short, it is possible to read all types of data sources into KNIME. We will take a closer look at this in the next chapter.

KNIME provides powerful and flexible tools for importing and accessing data from a wide variety of sources, whether you're working with flat files, relational databases, cloud platforms, or NoSQL systems

1.) Importing Flat Files

If you need to import flat files, KNIME offers dedicated nodes for various formats, including:

- Text and CSV files
- Excel files
- SAS files

2.) Accessing Relational Databases

For querying relational databases, KNIME includes specialized database connector nodes for:

- MySQL
- Oracle
- SQLite
- Snowflake
- PostgreSQL
- H2
- Microsoft Access
- Microsoft SQL Server

KNIME also supports connections to cloud-based databases such as Google BigQuery and Amazon Redshift.

When it comes to querying these databases, you have two options:

1. **Write SQL queries** directly within a node, offering full control for experienced users.

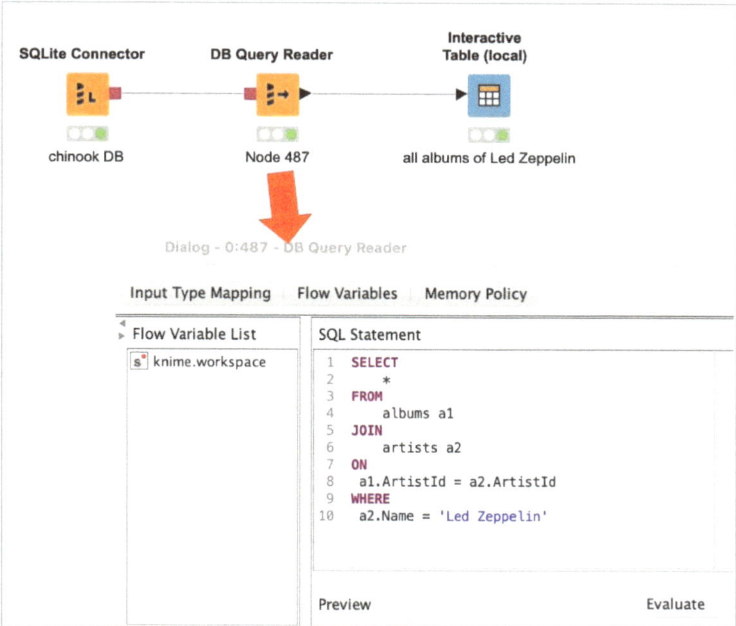

Fig. 4.11 Querying a database in KNIME with SQL

2. **Use preconfigured DB nodes** that allow you to build queries visually, ideal for those with limited SQL experience.

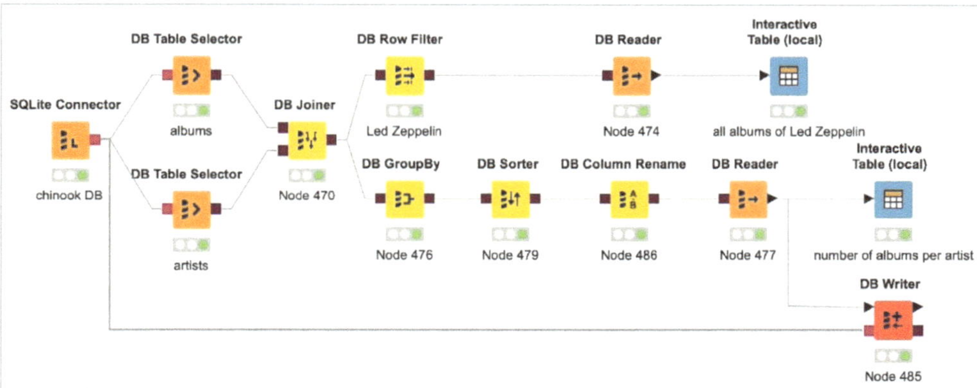

Fig. 4.12 Querying a database in KNIME with the DB Nodes

3.) Accessing NoSQL Databases

KNIME supports NoSQL databases as well, such as MongoDB, which can be accessed through dedicated nodes for working with JSON and similar data formats.

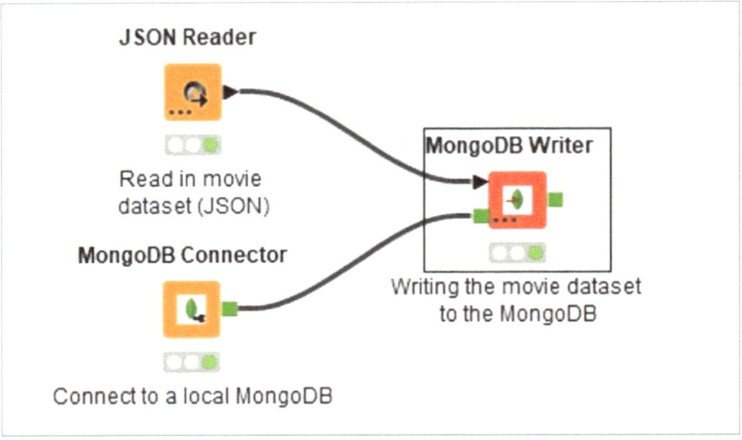

Fig. 4.13 Loading JSON dataset in MongoDB

And best of all, KNIME lets you combine data from all these sources into a single workflow. This enables seamless integration across different systems, regardless of whether you are merging data from MySQL, MongoDB, SQL Server, MariaDB, Oracle or PostgreSQL into a coherent analysis pipeline.

Machine Learning

KNIME offers a comprehensive suite of machine learning algorithms, enabling users to build powerful models with ease. Some of the key algorithms available in KNIME include:

1.) Supervised learning algorithms

These include widely used methods such as Linear, Polynomial, and Logistic Regression, Generalized Linear Models (GLM), Regression Trees, Random Forest, Support Vector Machines (SVMs), and Neural Networks.

2.) Unsupervised learning algorithms

Algorithms like K-Means Clustering, Principal Component Analysis (PCA), and Hierarchical Clustering are available for exploratory analysis and pattern discovery.

3.) Semi-supervised learning algorithms

KNIME supports methods such as Self-Organizing Maps (SOMs) and Expectation Maximization (EM) for working with partially labeled data.

4.) Ensemble learning algorithms

Techniques like Bagging, Boosting, and Random Subspace help improve model accuracy by combining multiple learners.

5.) Deep learning algorithms

Advanced models such as Convolutional Neural Networks (CNNs) and Recurrent Neural Networks (RNNs), including Long Short-Term Memory (LSTM) networks, are also supported for complex tasks like image and sequence processing.

All of these algorithms can be seamlessly integrated into KNIME workflows using dedicated nodes, allowing users to design and deploy sophisticated machine learning solutions quickly and efficiently.

With KNIME, users can quickly and easily build, evaluate, and deploy machine learning models with minimal coding required.

HERE'S a link to a cheat sheet on machine learning along with tips and tricks:

https://www.knime.com/files/machine-learning-with-knime.pdf

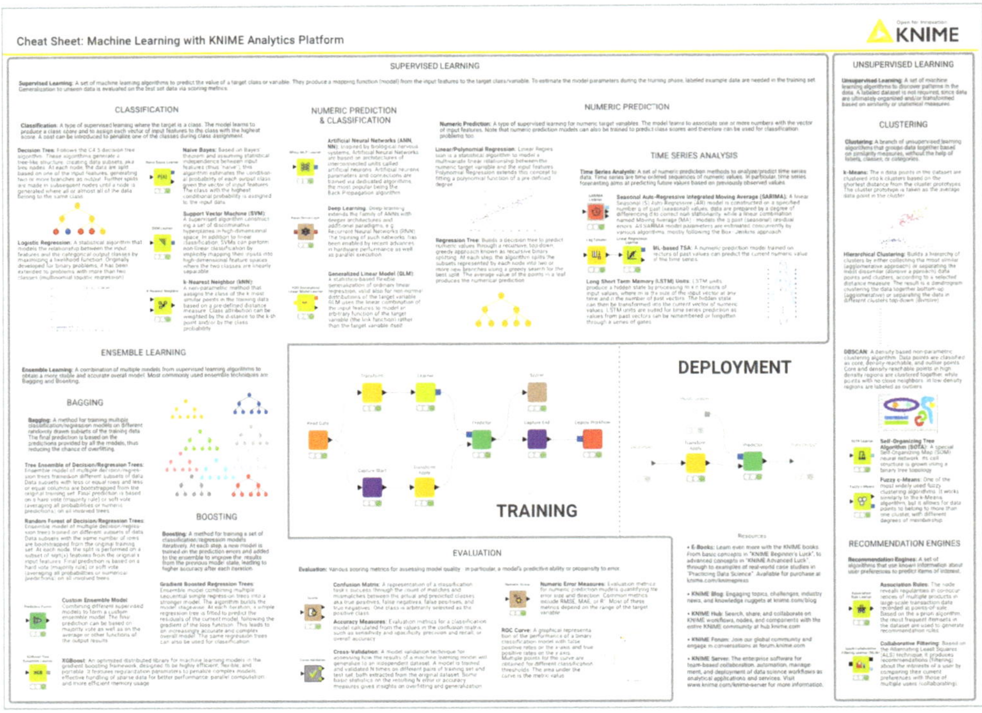

Fig. 4.14 KNIME cheat sheet for Machine Learning

Extensions for Python, R, and JavaScript

KNIME is a flexible and extensible platform that supports integration with popular programming languages such as Python and R.

This allows data scientists to use their preferred languages to build and deploy models directly within the KNIME environment, while also taking advantage of powerful libraries like TensorFlow, scikit-learn, and many others.

1.1) Python Integration in KNIME

As of KNIME Platform 4.7 and later, Python integration comes with a bundled environment that includes a selection of commonly used libraries. This setup lets you use the **Python Script** node out of the box, with no need to manually install or configure a Python environment.

1.2) Adding Custom Python Packages

When additional Python packages are needed, KNIME provides a solution through the **Conda Environment Propagation** node. This node captures your Python environment, including installed packages or the environment name, and applies it to other execution locations where Conda is available. Configuration is simple: select the environment and specify the required packages directly in the node.

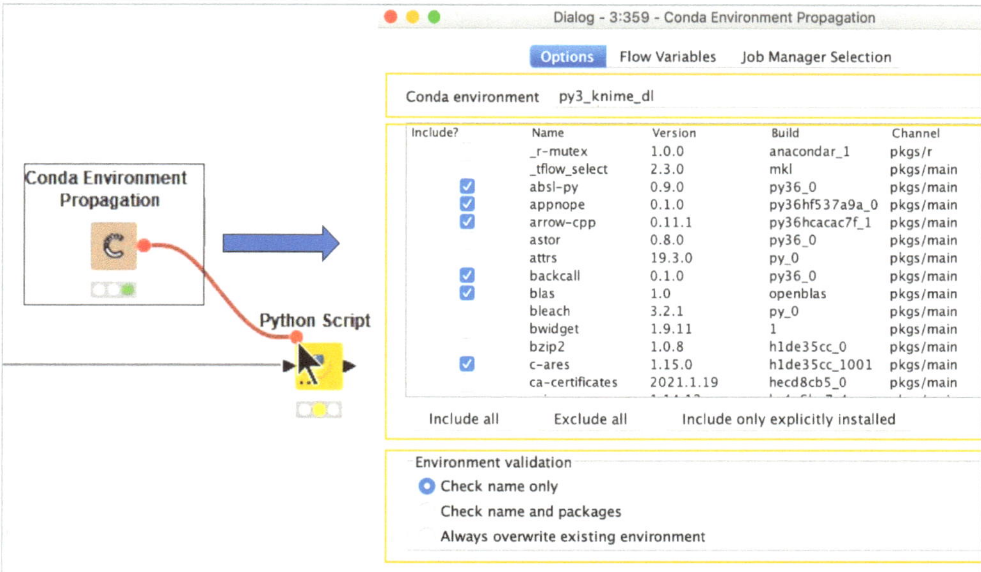

Fig. 4.15 The **Conda Environment Propagation** node

1.3) Python Script Space on the KNIME Community Hub

To help users get started, the **Python Script Space** on the KNIME Community Hub offers a collection of example workflows. These examples are especially useful for those who want to incorporate Python scripting into their KNIME projects and learn through practical, ready-to-use cases.

https://hub.knime.com/s/1_0f6fdjqeLPCfPY

2.) R Integration in KNIME

KNIME supports R through the extension **KNIME Interactive R Statistics Integration**. After installing it from the Extensions menu, you need to configure KNIME by specifying your local R installation (via **File → Preferences → KNIME → R**). This enables nodes like **R Snippet**, **R View**, and **R Learner**, allowing you to run R code, visualize results, and build models directly within KNIME workflows.

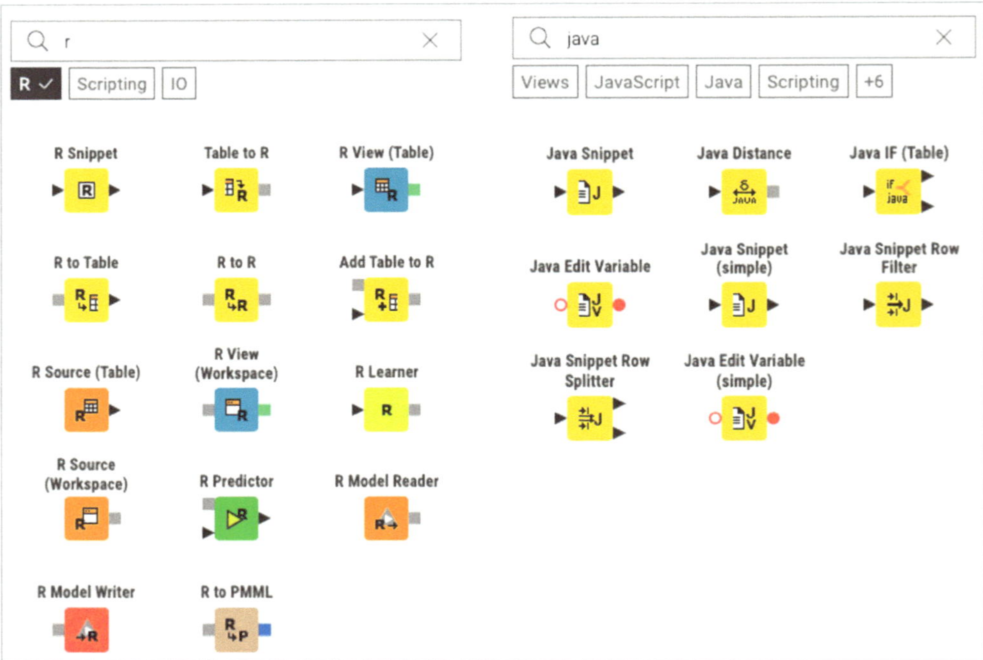

Fig. 4.16 R nodes and JavaScript nodes in KNIME

3.) JavaScript Integration in KNIME

JavaScript nodes come pre-installed in KNIME, requiring no additional setup. These nodes allow you to write and execute JavaScript code for custom data processing and manipulation directly within your workflows.

AI extension

Data science has taken a giant leap forward with the arrival of **Large Language Models**, and KNIME is right there at the forefront of this transformation. What once took hours of coding and complex logic can now be done with a well-crafted prompt.

KNIME's AI extensions make it incredibly easy to tap into the power of models like GPT or Hugging Face Transformers, right inside your workflow. Whether you're summarizing documents, generating text, building smart assistants, or just exploring unstructured data in a whole new way, KNIME brings the magic of generative AI to your fingertips.

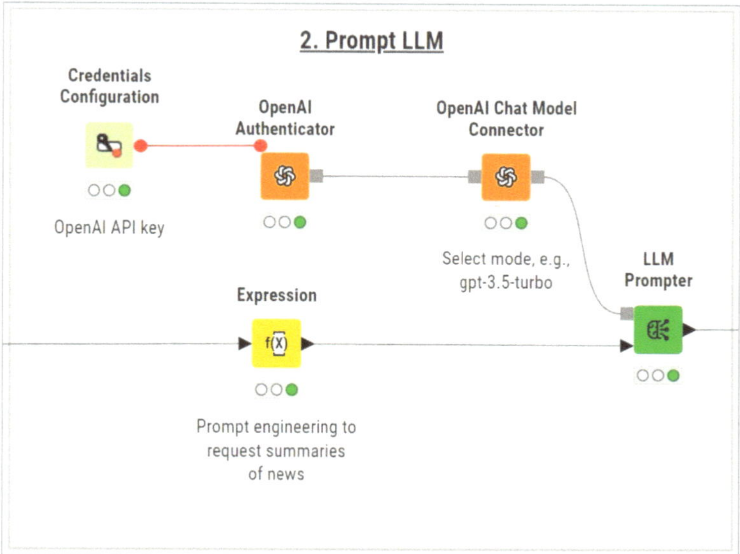

Fig. 4.17 KNIME LLM Extension

It's exciting, it's powerful, and it's yet another reason why KNIME will continue to be the best kept secret in modern data science.

Given the breadth and depth of AI capabilities, this topic warrants its own dedicated book to fully explore all the possibilities.

5

KNIME IN ACTION

"Theory is good, but practice is better," as the old saying goes. So let's jump straight into a few examples to see how you can use KNIME in real-world scenarios.

While not all workflows are based on real-life datasets, they reflect typical challenges faced in day-to-day work. These examples are designed to help business analysts, data engineers, and data analysts understand how to use KNIME for everyday data tasks. Covering a variety of fields and use cases, the workflows serve as a hands-on guide for applying KNIME to solve real business problems.

All the KNIME workflows discussed in this book are available in my **KNIME Community Hub space**, ***The KNIME Way***. You can find them here:

https://hub.knime.com/s/YDl1dMbgfzkNVOYO

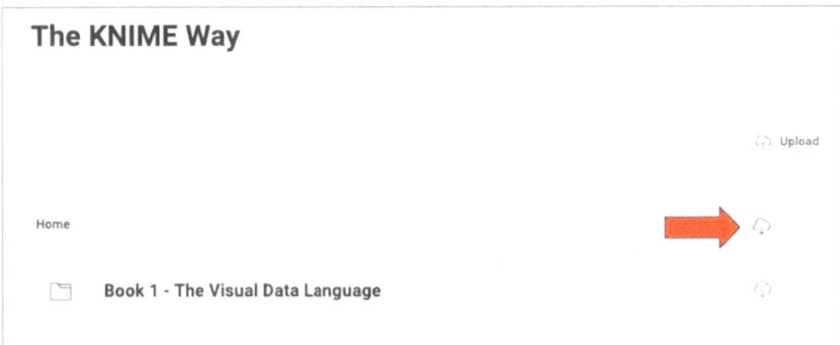

Fig. 5.1 **The KNIME Way** space on the Community Hub

To download the files for this book, click on "**Download folder**" (see red arrow). A file with the name "**Book 1 - The Visual Data Language.knar**" will then be downloaded.

To import this file into KNIME and run through all examples, open KNIME and select the "**Local Space**" and then import the download file by clicking on "**Import workflow**".

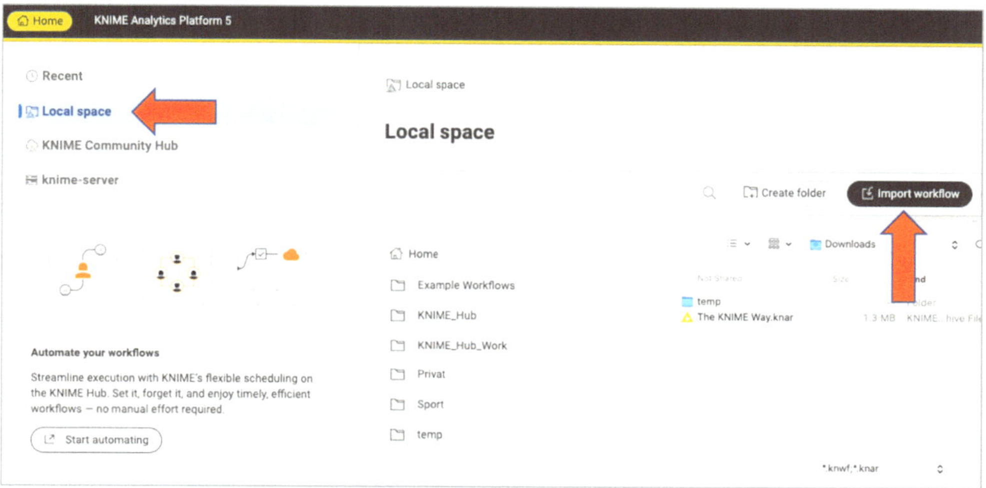

Fig. 5.2 Import example files in KNIME

You should now see a directory called "**Book 1 - The Visual Data Language**" in the "Local Space". When you open it, the different parts of the book will appear, and you will also find all the example workflows.

These KNIME workflows offer a practical introduction to essential tasks such as data integration, ETL, analysis, and reporting. Each workflow provides hands-on experience through real-world data scenarios and clear, step-by-step instructions.

Below is an overview of the example workflows included:

1. **Personal Finance: Tracking Spending with KNIME & Excel** - Learn how to import and analyze your personal expenses using KNIME integrated with Excel, helping you get a clear picture of your spending habits.
2. **Sales Reporting: From Database to Dashboard** - Explore how to extract sales data from databases, transform it, and create insightful dashboards for effective business reporting.

3. **Weather Data: Is This Year Warmer? Looping Files & API Access -** Analyze weather data by looping through multiple files and accessing APIs to uncover trends and compare temperatures over time.
4. **Financial Data: Exporting Stock Prices via API -** Use KNIME workflows to retrieve and export stock price data via APIs, perfect for financial analysis and market tracking.
5. **Sports Analytics: Predicting Football Results with KNIME -** Apply predictive analytics techniques to football data to forecast match outcomes, blending sports passion with data science.
6. **Visualization with K-AI & Python: Recreating Minard's Chart -** Combine KNIME, K-AI, and Python to recreate one of the most famous data visualizations, illustrating complex data with elegant clarity.

Remember, mastery comes with practice and curiosity. Keep exploring and experimenting. Each challenge you tackle brings you closer to becoming a confident, capable analyst.

*You're on the right path: you're on the **KNIME way**.*

---

1. Personal Finance: Tracking Spending with KNIME & Excel

This has always been one of the most important KNIME workflows in my life. Over time, I've adapted it to changing circumstances.

Yes, because it's very important to track your personal spending in order to achieve your financial goals. This way, my wife and I not only managed to keep track of our expenses, but also to divide our annual budget so that we could always afford everything we needed and still save enough to fulfill all our wishes.

The aim of the following workflow is to merge different bank and credit card transaction files and bring them to a common denominator so that the expenses can be evaluated according to the same categories and currencies.

While you could do all of this in Excel, running through this example will show you just how much easier and more efficient it is in KNIME.

But now to my problem: I have a bank account in Switzerland and one in Italy. When I'm in Switzerland, I use the Swiss debit card and pay in Swiss francs (CHF). In Italy, I use the Italian card and pay in euros (EUR). I also use my credit card for online services and online shopping. The following diagram show schematically how the files are to be merged.

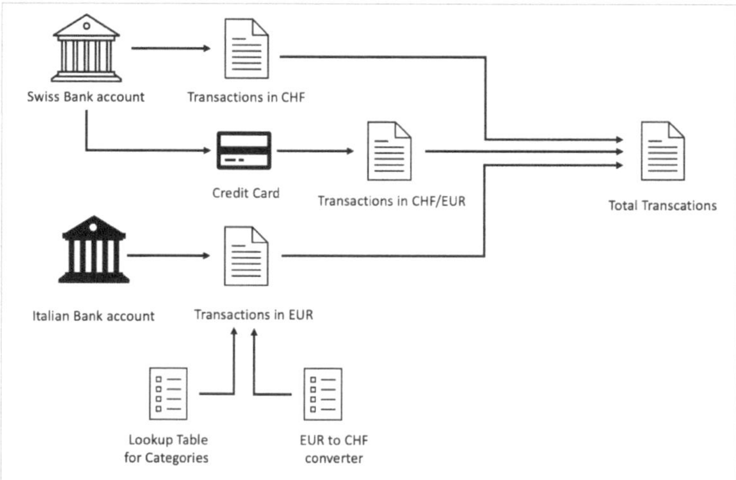

Fig. 5.3 Bank and Credit Card Transactions ETL

How can I now combine the monthly bank and credit card transactions so that the expenses are summarized according to the same categories and evaluated uniformly in CHF?

Since the Italian bank account uses a different categorization system for marking transactions, I will use a lookup table I created myself to match them with the Swiss transactions. I will also need to convert the euro amounts into Swiss francs using the exchange rate applicable on the day.

We will go through this example step by step, as it includes typical workflow steps that provide many beginners with an initial understanding of how to work with KNIME. For experienced KNIMErs, this is just repetition.

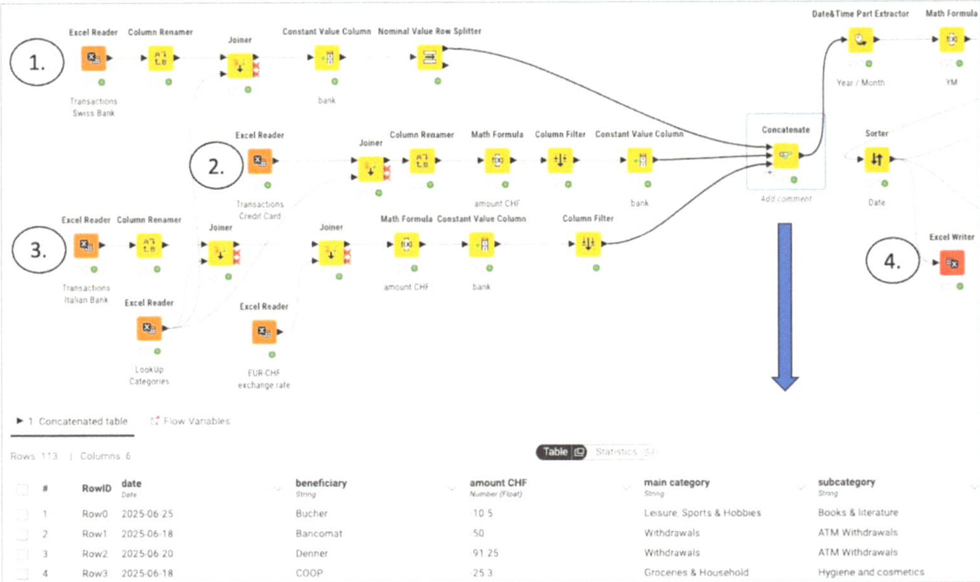

Fig. 5.4 KNIME Transactions ETL workflow

The KNIME workflow above fulfills all our requirements and is even similar to the diagram shown before.

Let's go through the corresponding steps:

1.) The Excel file containing transactions exported from the Swiss Bank account is first imported by double clicking the **Excel Reader** node. The column names are then renamed and translated into English.

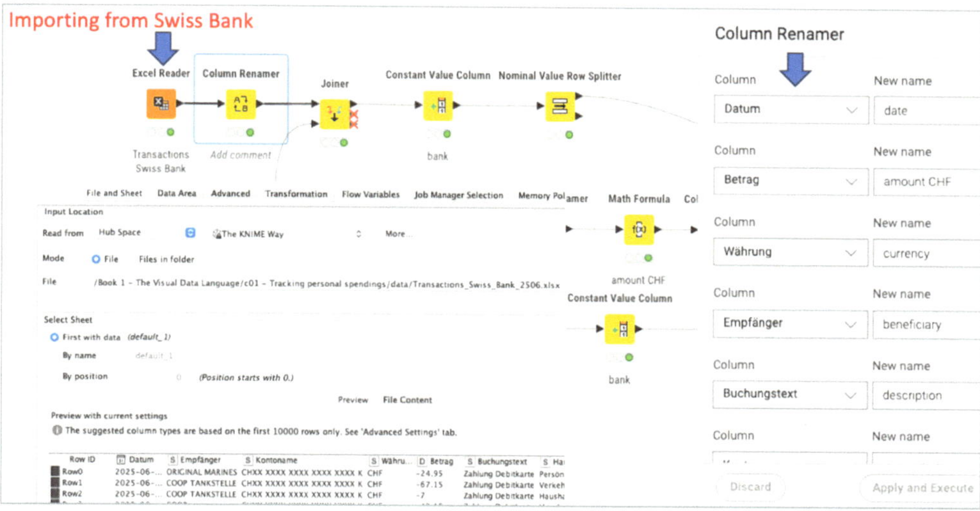

Fig. 5.5 Importing transactions from the Swiss Bank

Then the file is joined with a lookup table, which contains the categories in English using the two columns "Hauptkategorie" (= main category) and "Unterkategorie" (= subcategory). In the **Joiner** node, you can also select which columns you want to keep in the output column.

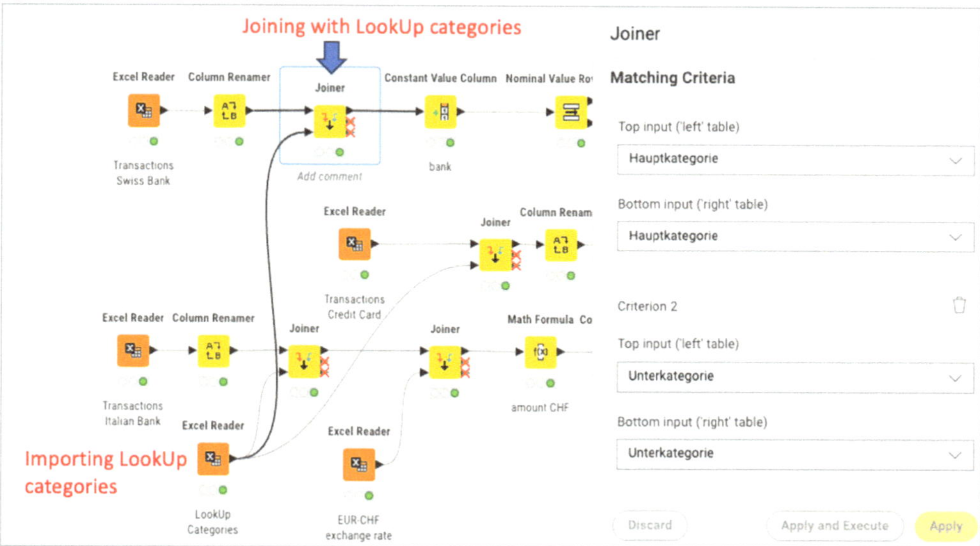

Fig. 5.6 Joining with the table LookUp categories

The **Constant Value** node adds a column with the value "Swiss Bank". This allows us to differentiate between the various transaction data. Next, only transactions that have been assigned a category are kept. This is because the uncategorized transaction represents the total of all credit card transactions, which are already included in a separate file described in (2.).

2.) The credit card transactions are imported separately, since they were filtered out in step 1. This table contains all credit card transactions along with their corresponding categories, allowing for more accurate tracking of expenses.

As with the transactions above, we join the „LookUp category" table and rename the columns in English. Then we calculate the „amount in CHF" by adding up the purchases and refunds.

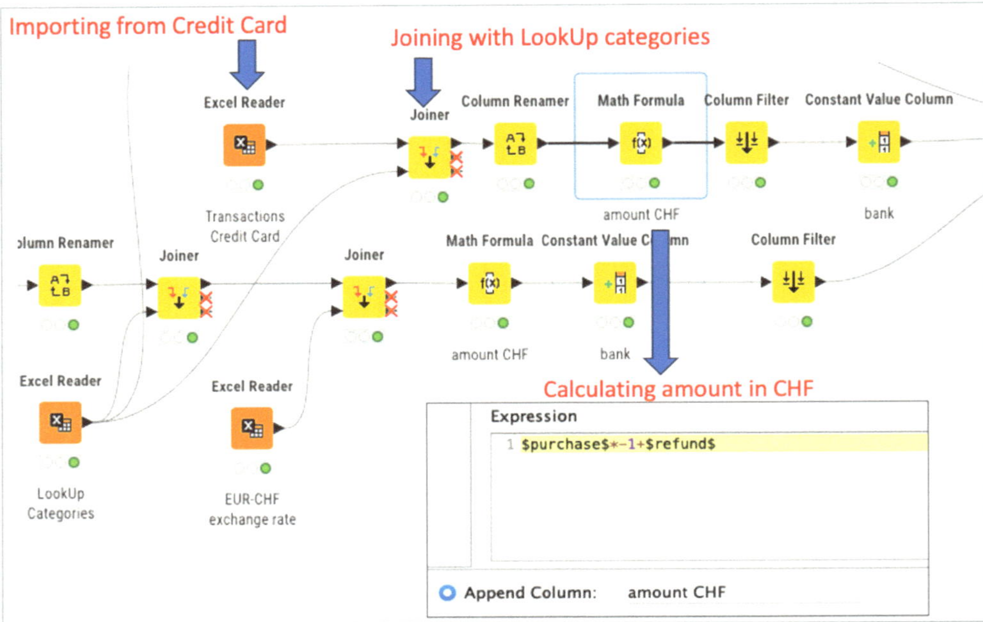

Fig. 5.7 Importing transactions from Credit Card

3.) Next, we process the transactions from the Italian Bank. Here is a special case. In the file exported from the online banking system, the transactions do not start until line 19, so this time we adjust the **Excel Reader** node so that we select line 19 as the first data line under "Data range" (see below).

The transactions are in euros this time, and their categories also need to be recoded. The two lookup tables, "LookUp categories" and "EUR to CHF exchange rate," are used to translate the categories and convert the transaction amounts from euros to Swiss francs.

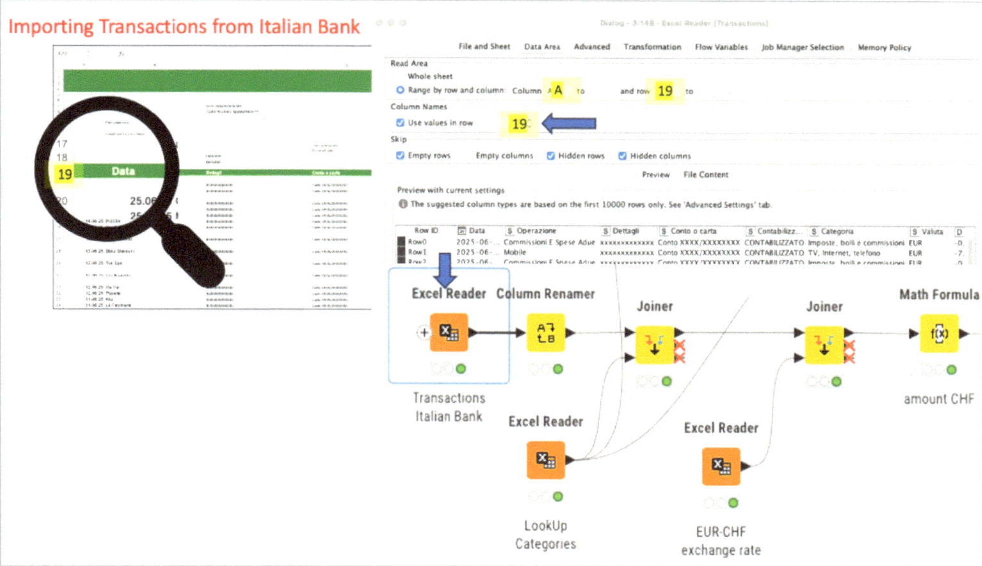

Fig. 5.8 Importing transactions from the Italian Bank

4.) Finally, all three tables are merged on the right-hand side of the workflow with the **Concatenate** node. If you click on the **Concatenate** node, you will see a table view of the data record in the lower part of the desktop. This is already our finalized data set, which we will use further in Excel.

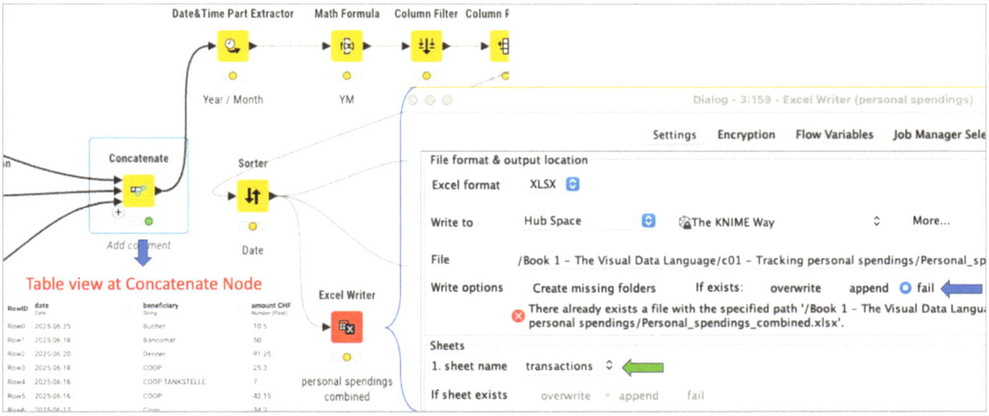

Fig. 5.9 Writing data in an Excel Sheet

Before we write out the Excel file, we use the **Date&Time Part Exctractor** node add the year extracted from the "date" column. We also calculate a column YM (YearMonth) which is made up of the year and the month. This makes it easier to track the history of transactions.

Things get interesting with the **Excel Writer** node, because it not only allows us to overwrite a sheet in an existing Excel file, but also to append new values to it.

The blue arrow lets you configure whether the entire Excel file should be overwritten. The green arrow allows you to set the same options for an individual sheet.

In this way, our pivot table created in Excel can always be updated with the latest data. Essentially, this setup provides us with a simple form of a database. This also makes it easier to compare manual entries such as planned values and budget values with the data updated from KNIME.

	A	B	C	D
4	**Categories**	**202505**	**202506**	**total**
5	**Communication & media**	**-64**	**-283**	**-346**
6	Electronic Devices & Accessories	-2	-51	-54
7	Multimedia (music, video & apps)	-21	-34	-55
8	Newspapers, Magazines & Subscriptions	-9		-9
9	Telephone, Internet & TV	-32	-198	-229
10	**Groceries & Household**	**-79**	**-1'911**	**-1'990**
11	Food & beverages		-1'524	-1'524
12	Household appliances		-286	-286
13	Household items and accessories	-79	-51	-130
14	Hygiene and cosmetics		-51	-51
15	**Housing & energy**	**-97**	**-219**	**-316**
16	Electricity & gas		-118	-118
17	Furnishings & furniture	-27	-5	-32
18	Tools & garden	-70	-97	-166
19	**Leisure, Sports & Hobbies**	**-55**	**-376**	**-432**
20	Books & literature	-31	-21	-52
21	Leisure, Culture & Movies		-355	-355
22	Website	-24		-24
23	**Other expenses**		**-35**	**-35**
24	Banking services		-35	-35
25	**Personal expenses**	**-47**	**-1'629**	**-1'676**
26	Clothing, shoes & accessories		-663	-663

transactions pivot +

Fig. 5.10 Excel Pivot table with spending by category

In this example, we have seen that KNIME and Excel can work together efficiently. KNIME takes care of the entire ETL process, while Excel serves as a flexible tool for visualization, manual data validation and further analysis.

KNIME isn't just for data engineers and scientists, it's also a powerful tool for business analysts! Its intuitive interface lets analysts prepare data for reporting, analysis, and decision-making, all without writing code.

2. Sales Reporting: From Database to Dashboard

Many small and medium-sized enterprises (SMEs) continue to rely on **Microsoft Access** or similar desktop database systems to manage their day-to-day operations, particularly for smaller-scale or legacy applications. These systems remain popular due to their ease of setup and familiarity, making them suitable for businesses without the need or resources for large-scale enterprise databases.

To analyze, report on, and extend the capabilities of such databases, **KNIME** offer powerful options for connecting to Access databases (and other **relational databases**), running queries, integrating data and building interactive dashboards.

One of the best-known sample databases for demonstrating these concepts is the **Northwind database** which models a fictional company called **Northwind Traders**, a wholesale food and beverage distributor.

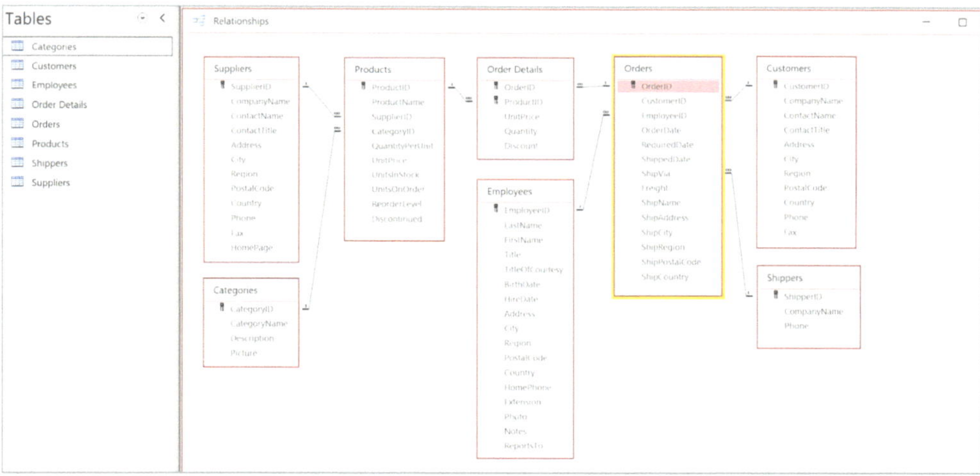

Fig. 5.11 ER diagram of Northwind database

This company purchases products from various suppliers and sells them to customers, mainly retailers or other businesses. The database is designed to reflect a typical business workflow involving inventory management, sales order processing, supplier relations, and employee roles.

The image shows the entity relationships of the database, illustrating how key entities such as Customers, Orders, Employees, Products, Suppliers, and Categories are connected through primary and foreign key relationships, providing a visual representation of the database structure.

Thanks to its clear structure and realistic sample data, Northwind serves as an ideal sandbox to show how KNIME's database nodes can connect to relational data sources, run queries, and build a simple executive dashboard. The process is similar for any relational SQL database.

As mentioned in Chapter 4, in the section *"Data Access with KNIME,"* there are dedicated nodes available to connect to any relational database. We load the Northwind database using the **Microsoft Access Connector** node. Then, the **DB Table Selector** node is used to choose specific tables or views created in Access.

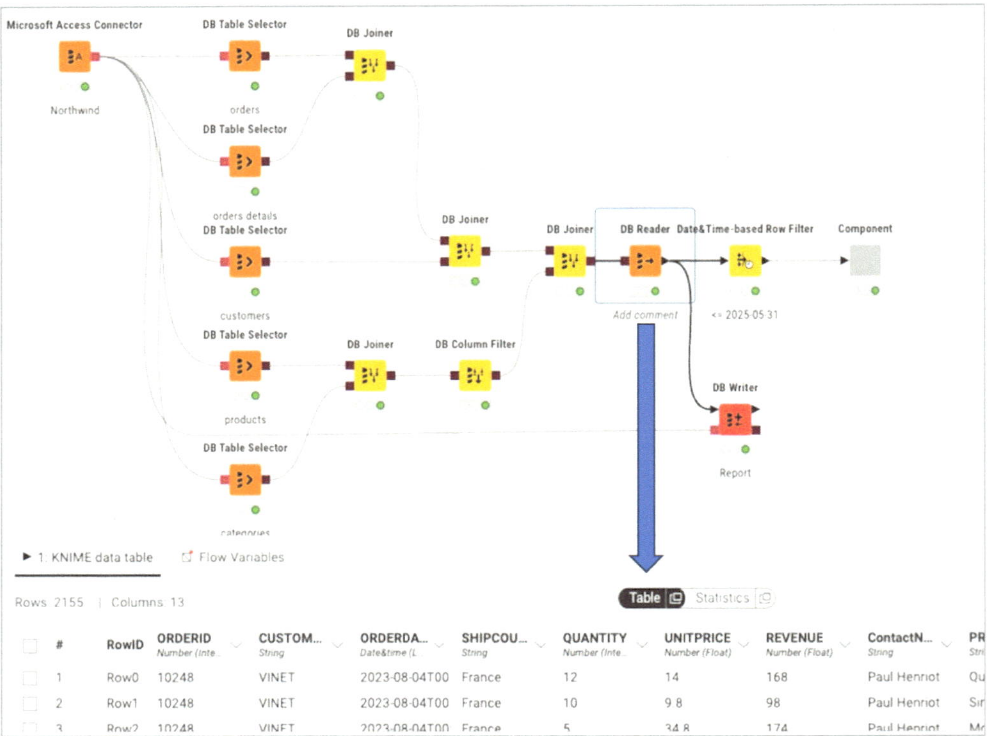

Fig. 5.12 KNIME workflow for Northwind Dashboard

The final table, which will be used to build the dashboard, should include order information along with revenues, customer names, product details, and their categories. We will then use this table to set up our dashboard.

In the **DB Table Selector** node, we can select the table we want to query from the database. Experienced SQL users can even write their own queries directly in the node. And after each step, you can retrieve between 100 and 5000 rows to check the content of the resulting table.

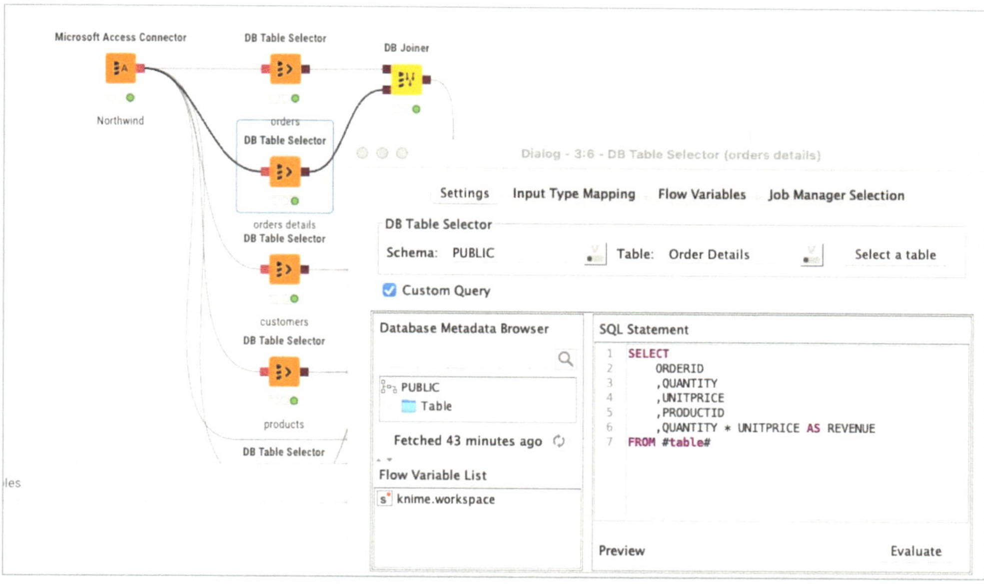

Fig. 5.13 The **DB Table Selector** node

We can retrieve most tables directly via this node without writing a line of SQL code. However, it is also possible to use SQL code. To demonstrate this we write a SQL code to calculate the revenue from orders quantity and unit price from the **Order Details** table.

We could also have done this with a node "outside" the database query, for example with the **Math Formula** node. But in many cases, databases are located on high-performance servers and it often makes more sense to execute the queries directly on the database before the final data is retrieved. This way, you need fewer resources on your own computer and can get the work done faster.

Therefore, we will also use the **DB Joiner** node to join the required tables. There are also other DB nodes that process the data directly in the database, such as the **DB Group By**, **DB Sorter**, etc. nodes.

Be careful when using these nodes to query your company's databases. Talk to your database administrator. Otherwise they could "punish" you quickly so that your queries are suddenly terminated.

To process the data outside the database in KNIME, we use the **DB Reader** Node. From here you can use the data with the usual nodes in KNIME.

Before we get to the report part, we save our generated file in a table of the same database. We create a new table in the database called **Report**.

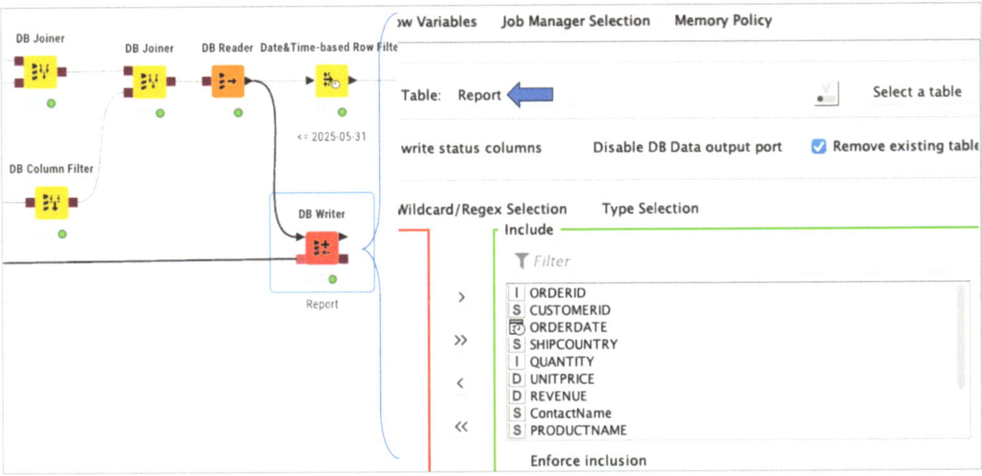

Fig. 5.14 Writing data to Database with the **DB Writer** node

The next node is a component. To open the **Component** node, it is not enough to double-click it, you open it by right-clicking on it and selecting **Component/Open Component.**

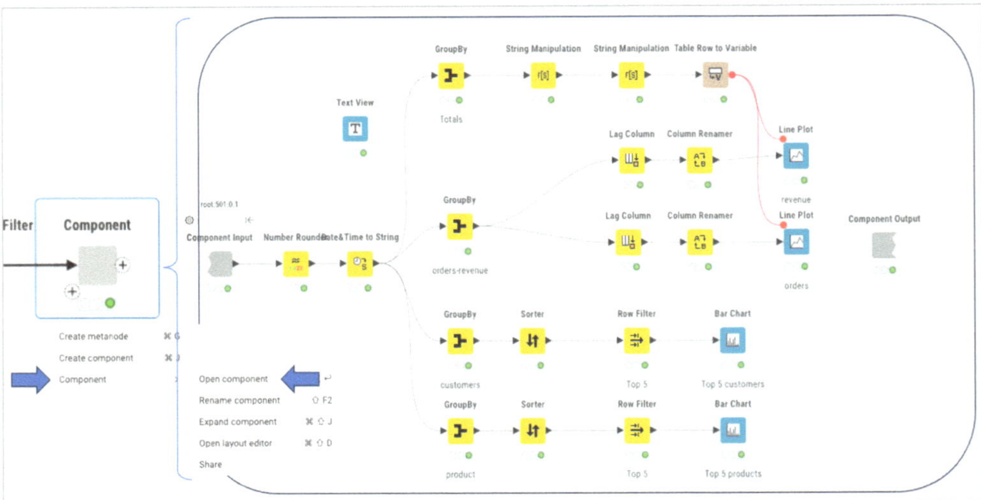

Fig. 5.15 **Component** with Reporting workflow

A **Component** in KNIME is a container that groups multiple nodes together to perform a specific task. To create a component, select the desired nodes of the workflow and right-click on "Create Component".

Components are reusable building blocks. They can be integrated across various workflows or shared with others. Their power lies in flexibility. Customizable inputs and outputs allow components to adapt seamlessly to different contexts and use cases.

In this example, the component is used to create a dashboard by combining the necessary data processing and visualization node into one task. Let's take a closer look inside this component:

First we calculate the two **KPI's** (Key Performance Indicators) **Total Revenue** and **Total Orders** with a **Group By** node and aggregate the sum of the values. Since we also use these values in the title of the associated line plots, we pass them on in a variable through the **Table Row to Variable** node.

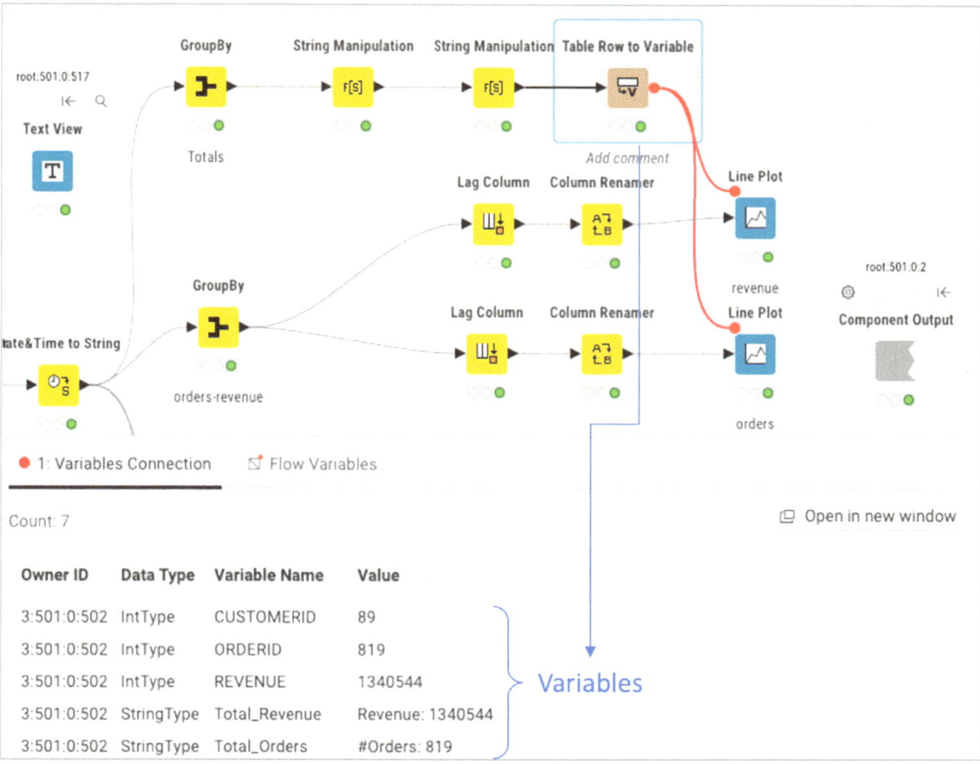

Fig. 5.16 Passing values through the **Table Row to Variable** node

This introduces a new concept. Previously, our work involved transforming data directly from tables that were always clearly visible in the workflow.

Now, similar to how variables are used in common programming languages, values are extracted and passed through nodes. These values travel on the red connections and can then be reused in different contexts – for example, to display a title on a chart. In the next step, we will see how we can integrate this variable into the line plot.

Since we want to compare the current revenues with the previous year's values in the line plot, we use:

1. A **Lag Column** node to shift the values by 12 months and create a new column **Revenue(-12)** representing the prior year's data.

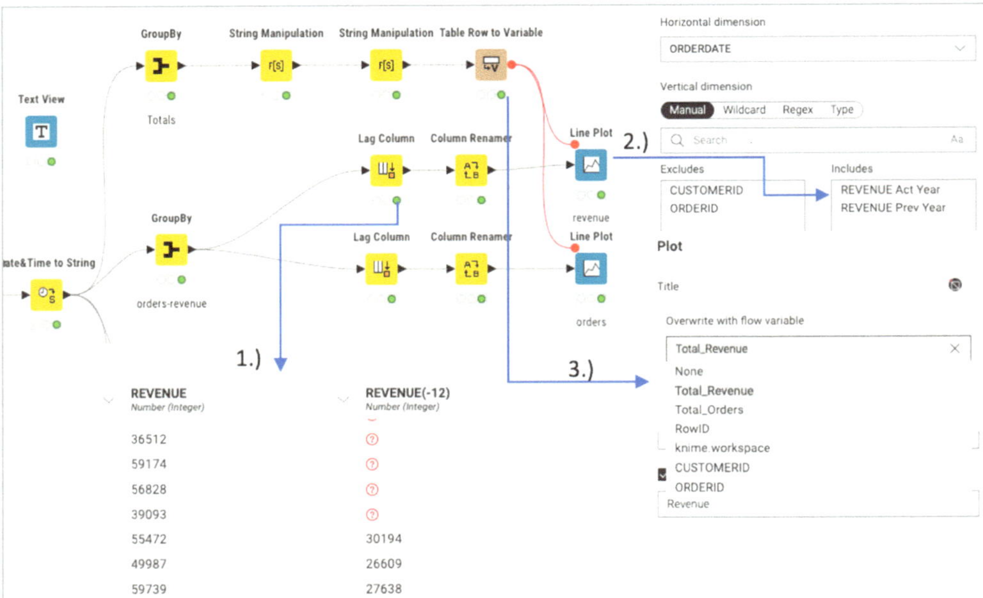

Fig. 5.17 Building a Line Plot with the revenues

2. We then add the revenues to the **Line Plot** menu and select the **Order date** as the horizontal dimension.
3. The previously created variable, which was formed from the total revenues, is used as the title for the Line Plot.

The line plot for orders is generated using the same approach. In addition, we create bar charts showing the 5 most important customers and the 5 most important products.

The following figure shows the final dashboard, which is displayed via the **Component** node after executing it.

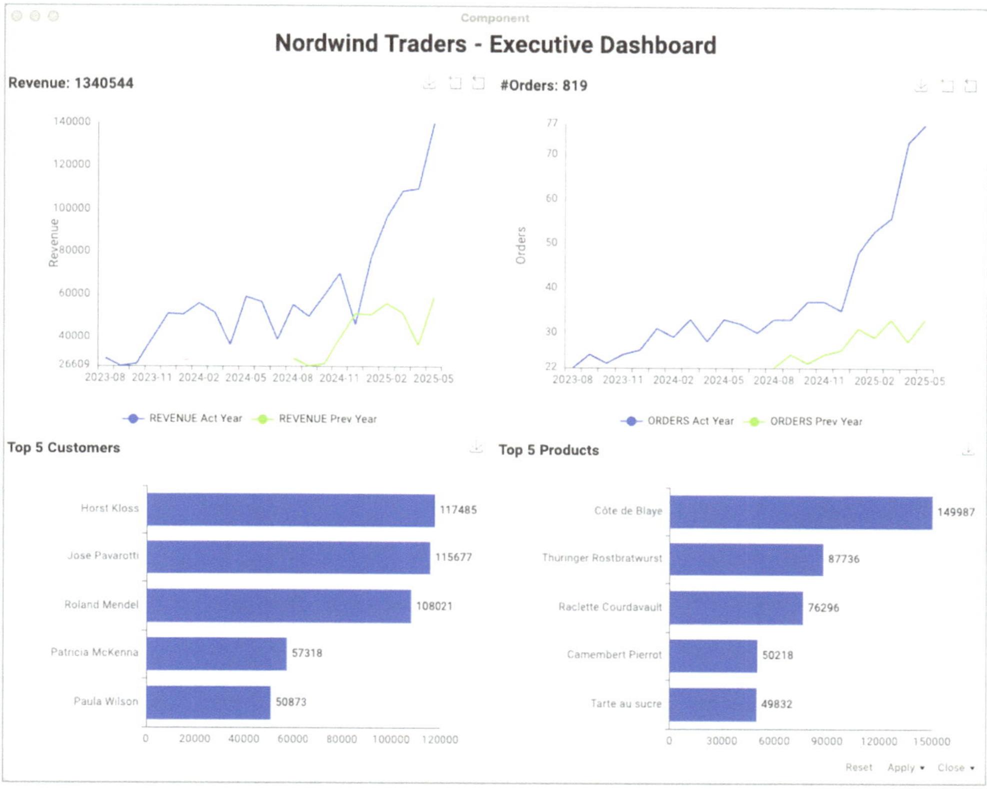

Fig. 5.18 The Northwind Traders - Executive Dashboard

Reports can be exported in formats such as PDF, HTML, and Excel, and automated report generation can be seamlessly integrated into your workflows. KNIME also enables easy data export, for example as CSV files, allowing you to transfer results to external tools like **Tableau**, **Power BI**, or other business intelligence platforms.

In fact, in our company, we successfully used the approach of exporting data to **Tableau** to share dashboards across the entire organization. This strategy significantly improved transparency and decision-making at all levels.

To explore the full range of reporting capabilities, make sure to check out the KNIME documentation, example workflows, cheatsheets, and learning resources available through the KNIME Community Hub (see Chapter 4 - Learning Resources). These materials provide practical guidance and inspiration for building advanced reporting solutions.

3. Weather Data: Is This Year Warmer? Looping Files & API Access

Two and a half years ago, my wife and I moved from Switzerland to Italy and settled in a small village nestled in the heart of the Po Valley where my parents once grew up. Our decision was driven by several factors - one of the most important being the climate.

In fact, spring and fall are fantastic here. Summer, on the other hand, is hot,... very hot. Because this place is mostly farming, the weather really matters for the crops. And with summers being so hot, everyone's saying this year is even hotter than the last.

I wouldn't say this year is hotter - on average, temperatures have been about the same as last year. Some months were hotter, others cooler, which leads to some pretty heated debates. But I've got my reasons. Since we moved here, I've been tracking the temperatures every week because they affect our heating bills in winter and how livable the summer will be.

Every week, I downloaded the weather data from the following Italian website https://www.ilmeteo.it/ and saved it as a CSV file in a dedicated directory. Let's see what I've found out.

We've already seen that there's nothing easier than reading a file in KNIME. But what about reading several files at once? How is that supposed to work? This is where you realize that we're working with a visual programming language, one that includes features like loops.

To read all the saved CSV files of the weather data in KNIME, use a **List Files/Folders** node. It retrieves the file paths, which you can then pass to a **Table Row to Variable Loop Start** node.

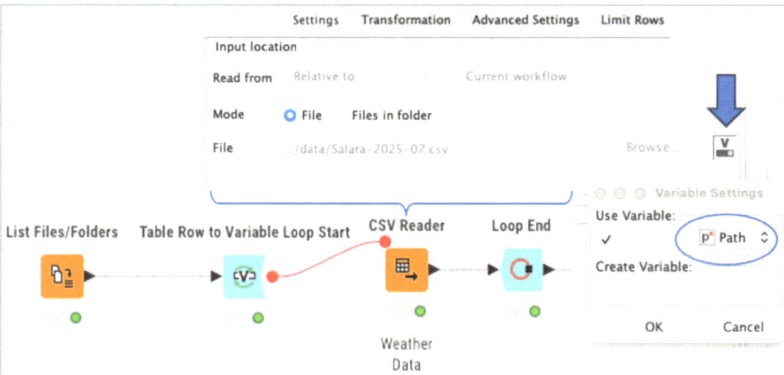

Fig. 5.19 Looping through CSV files with weather data

Inside the loop, use a **CSV Reader** to read each file for further processing. This time, instead of browsing for the file as usual, the file **path** is passed as a variable (see image). The loop does the rest and iterates through all available files. This way, all 19 files are loaded and combined into one dataset in just a short time.

With the **Rename** node, we translate the column names into English. Then, we use the **String to Date&Time** node to correctly format the date column.

In the image you see the configuration dialog of this node. Every KNIME node has its own settings menu where you can define specific operations and adjust parameters as needed.

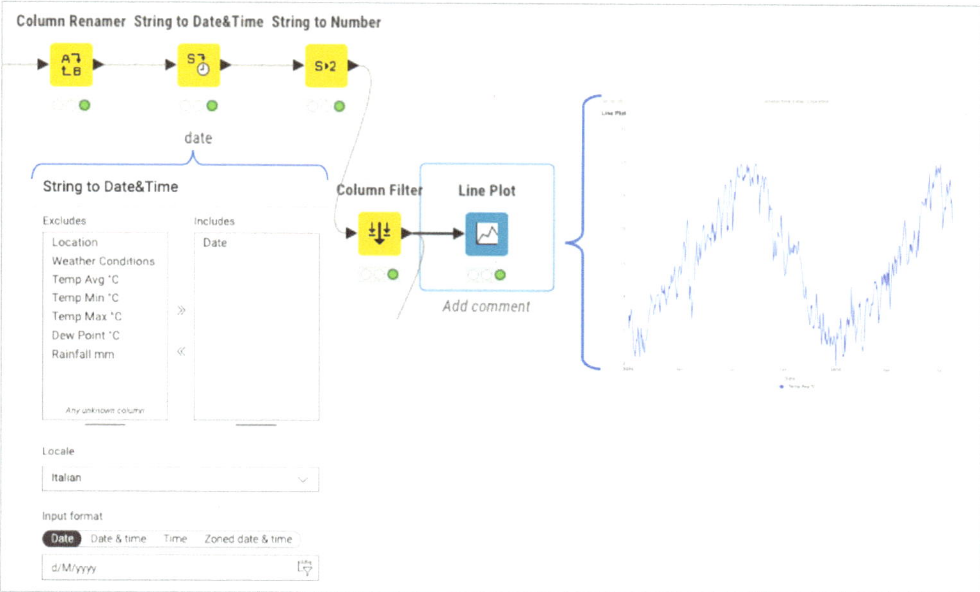

Fig. 5.20 Line Plot of temperatures since 2024

Next, we use the **String to Number** node to convert temperature values by replacing commas with decimal points, ensuring they are correctly interpreted as numbers.

This is incredibly helpful. Imagine having to search and replace all those values manually in Excel. One node does the work of many clicks.

Finally, we plot the temperatures since January 2024.

At first glance, nothing unusual stands out. Last year's temperature fluctuations appear to be repeating, with no significant differences observed.

To examine this more closely, we use a **Lag Column** node, just like in the previous Sales Report example, to create a comparison column showing values from the past 366 days, accounting for the leap year in 2024.

We then keep only the data from January 2025 and later, so the lag column's last year's values align for proper comparison. This is done using the **Date&Time-based Row Filter** node.

Now we want to compare how the data evolves over time, first by week and then by month. KNIME provides a convenient node for this purpose. The **Date&Time to String** node allows us to format date values according to the desired time granularity. We format the date as **yyyy-ww** to compare the temperatures by weeks, and as **yyyy-MM** to compare it by months.

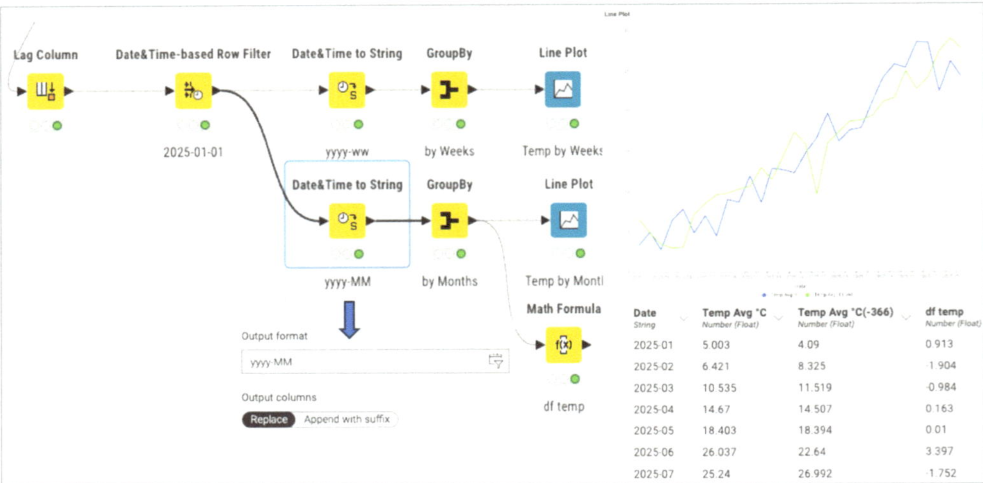

Fig. 5.21 Comparing temperature differences by week and by month

In the image the two evolutions of the temperatures (in green last year) show that hot periods change from last year to this year.

Same picture also for the months: February was hotter last year, June this year. The image above shows the temperature trends over time, with last year's data in green.

It highlights that the periods of heat have shifted between last year and this year. The monthly comparison tells a similar story: February was warmer last year, June has been hotter this year, and July so far is cooler than last year.

Comparing the two years up to this point, we see a **difference of just 0.038 degrees**. So, what happened with climate change?

To answer this question, we need more data from the past few years. But since I'm a bit lazy, I've found a new way to avoid manually gathering it.

By the way, I believe that, deep down, many data scientists are a bit lazy. Otherwise, they wouldn't choose a career in data science, where shortcuts and easy solutions seem to be everywhere. But, unfortunately, the reality is often quite different.

The website **open-meteo.com** seems perfect for my needs, offering historical weather data from all over the world. To use it, you just need to enter two geographic parameters: longitude and latitude, along with your desired date range. It also provides a variety of weather data, such as wind speed, precipitation, and more.

The data from your selection can be downloaded as an Excel or CSV file, but we only need the API URL, not the file, so we can import everything directly into KNIME.

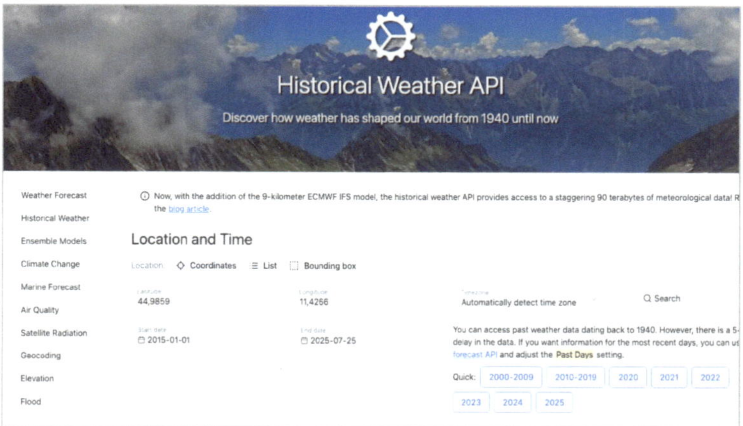

Fig. 5.22 Input mask on open-meteo.com

Furthermore, I want to compare the temperature trends over the last 20 years, ensuring the analysis is representative of all of Italy. Therefore, I will include data from 13 cities across the country. This means I need the longitude and latitude values for all of these cities.

Since I also want to automate this process, I will use an extension that includes a node for automatically generating these geo-coordinates: the **Geospatial Analytics Extension for KNIME.**

To install the extension, go to the KNIME **Menu**, then select **Install Extensions**. In the search field, type "Geospatial" and then check the **Geospatial Analytics Extension**.

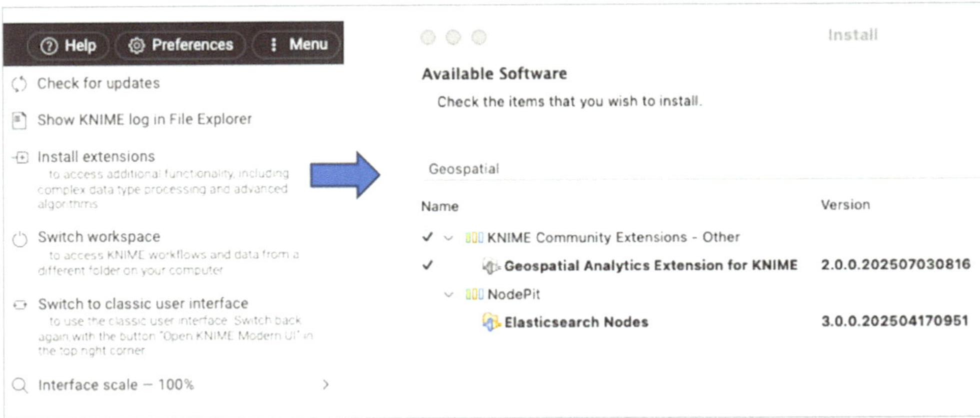

Fig. 5.23 Install extension in KNIME

After the installation you got new nodes to work on. One of them is the **OSM Boundary Map Table** node. This node is used to extract information from **OpenStreetMap** data, such as country borders, city boundaries, postal code areas, and their associated longitude and latitude coordinates. Simply input the city name, and everything is calculated automatically.

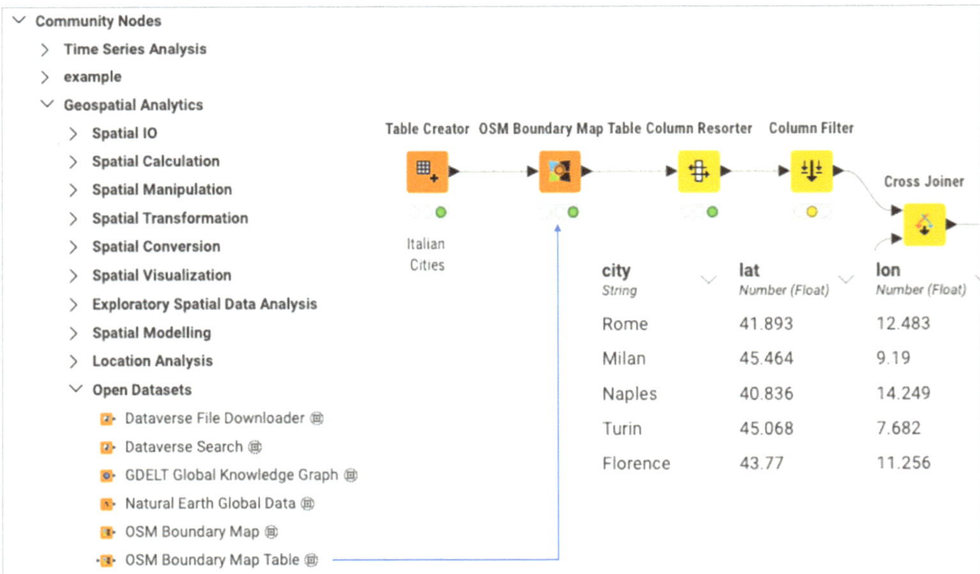

Fig. 5.24 City name to latitude and longitude resolution

By the way, the possibilities for using the Geospatial Analysis Nodes in KNIME are far from exhausted. This extension provides a wide range of powerful tools for spatial data processing, visualization, and analysis beyond what has been covered here.

Now, let's return to our weather data from open-meteo.com. To determine the required temperature data, we will only need to adjust the longitude and latitude data and the start and end dates. The following figure shows where the corresponding values can be found in the URL.

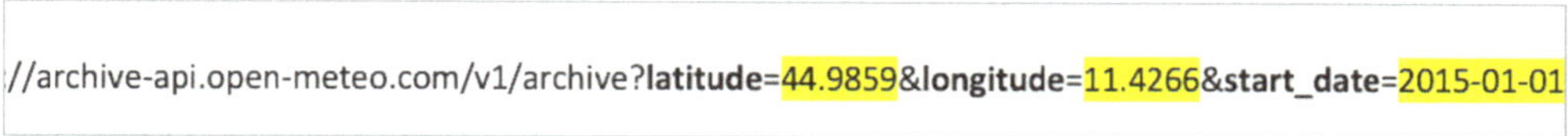

Fig. 5.25 Generated API URL

The first step is to load a table containing city names along with their corresponding geographical coordinates and join it with a separate table that holds the start and end dates for data retrieval. The **Cross Joiner** node merges both tables, enabling us to loop through each city and retrieve the corresponding weather data.

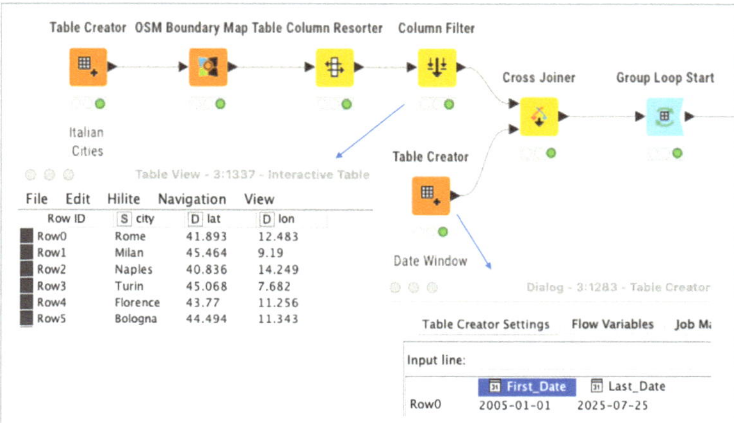

Fig. 5.26 Cross join of the two tables

The **Cross Joiner** node in KNIME performs a **Cartesian product** (also called a **cross join**) between two input tables. This means it combines every row from the first table with every row from the second table, resulting in a new table where each row is a combination of one row from each input.

The second step involves **setting up a loop** over all cities with the desired API call to automate the data collection process.

The following four nodes handle most of the work: The **String Manipulation** node generates the URL path using the geographical coordinates of the corresponding Italian city.

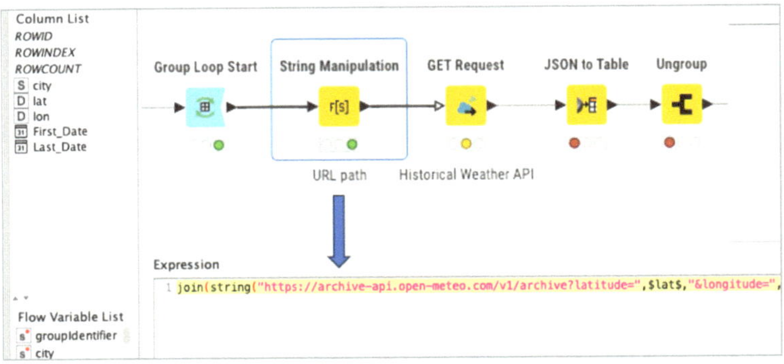

Fig. 5.27 Creating the API call with the **String Manipulation** node

The **GET Request** node sends the URL path to the open-meteo API and retrieves a JSON file containing all the necessary information. (Do not forget to set an appropriate delay (ms) of at least 100.)

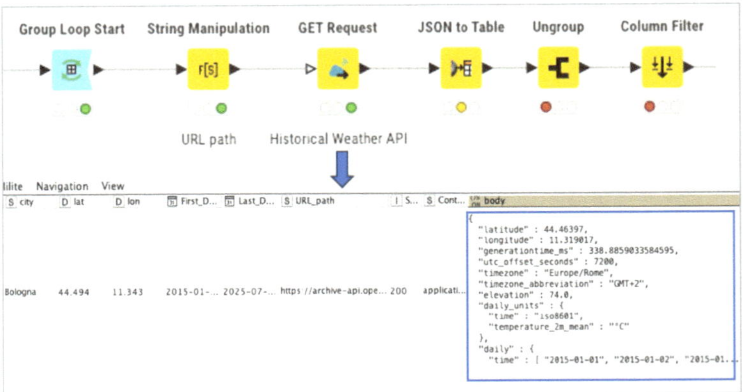

Fig. 5.28 The **GET Request** node sends request to API

Next, we need to convert this JSON data into a usable format. Fortunately, KNIME provides an efficient solution for this. The **JSON to Table** node transforms the JSON column into a table format, while the **Ungroup** node finally organizes the data into separate columns for dates and the corresponding weather information.

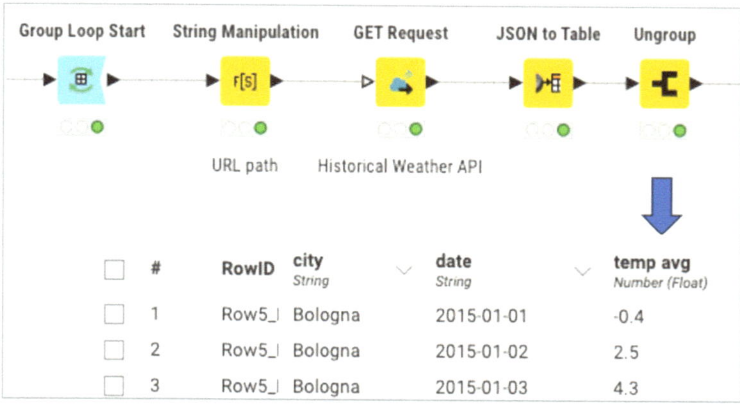

Fig. 5.29 Converting JSON column to suitable table

Finally, the consolidated weather data for all Italian cities, across the entire date range, is written to a CSV file.

Now, we load the data for each city using a **CSV Reader** node and plot the yearly temperature. To get a line for every city, we need to transform the data with a **Pivot** node. This node reshapes the dataset by turning city names into separate columns, with the temperature values in each column, allowing us to compare temperature trends across all cities in a single, clear visualization.

Fig. 5.30 Temperature Trends in Italy (2005–2025)

An upward trend is starting to emerge, but the overall picture becomes much clearer when we analyze the average values across all cities combined. The data confirm a consistent long-term warming pattern.

4. Financial Data: Exporting Stock Prices via API

Yahoo Finance was once known for providing direct, user-friendly access to financial data through downloadable CSV files, making it easy for analysts and developers to work with historical stock data.

While the official public API was discontinued around 2017, the ability to download CSV files directly from the website remained available until at least 2022.

However, in 2023, Yahoo Finance introduced a paywall restricting access to this feature. Users without a premium subscription began encountering messages indicating that downloading historical data was only available to Gold members.

Yahoo Finance does not offer an official public API anymore for downloading stock data; however, you can still access Yahoo Finance data through unofficial means, as it still exposes a downloadable CSV endpoint for historical data. Here is an example with the Apple stock:

https://query2.finance.yahoo.com/v8/finance/chart/AAPL?period1=1640995200&period2=1753488000&interval=1d

---

Disclaimer: Please note that the methods and solutions described in this book are based on the current state of available tools and services. It is possible that after the publication of this book, these solutions may no longer function due to changes in policies, APIs, or service availability. Readers are encouraged to verify the latest information and adapt accordingly.

In this example we will collect daily data for three selected stocks from the last tree and a half years:

- NVidia (NVDA)
- Apple (AAPL)
- Google (GOOG)

In the previous weather example, we saw that the start and end dates could be provided in a regular date format. In this case, however, the UNIX date format is used to select the data.

This means that we will first convert the start and end dates of the API call into UNIX format, and then revert them to the standard date format after retrieving the data. Since we will need a few nodes for this, we pack everything in a metanode to keep the workflow organized.

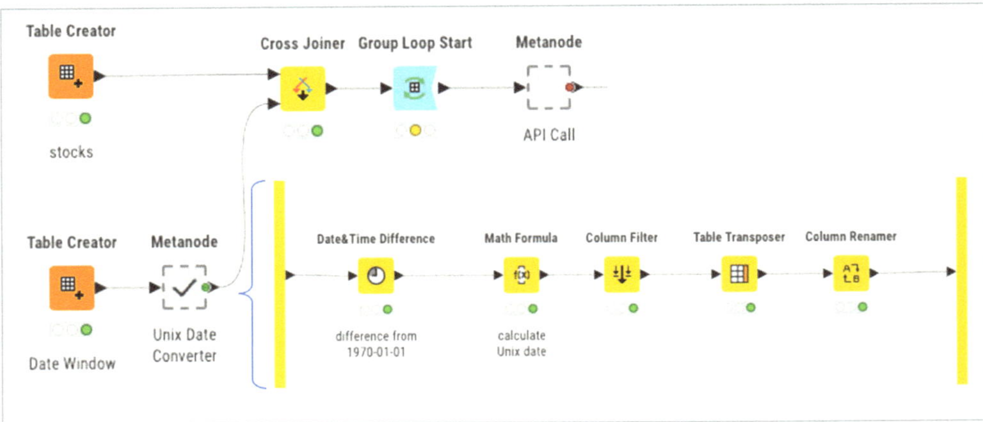

Fig. 5.31 Metanode with Unix date converter

To convert a date in KNIME (e.g., 2023-01-03) to a **Unix timestamp** (seconds since Jan 1, 1970) use the **Date&Time Difference** node to calculate the number of days between your date and 1970-01-01. Then, multiply the resulting number of days by **86400** (the number of seconds in a day) to obtain the Unix timestamp.

Next, we perform a cross join, similar to the approach used in our previous weather example.

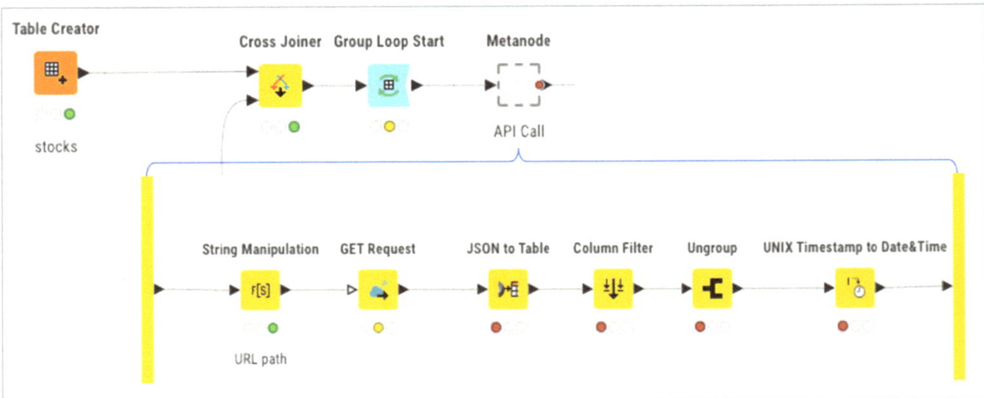

Fig. 5.32 Metanode with API call

Inside the following **Metanode API Call**, we use a **String Manipulation** node to construct the desired URL. This time, we need to append a **Unix Timestamp to Date&Time** node at the end to convert the Unix timestamp back into a standard date format.

To help identify potential buy and sell signals, we include two widely used technical indicators: the 50-day and 200-day **Simple Moving Averages** (SMA).

Here's a brief detour into **technical analysis**:

A **golden cross** is a **bullish** signal in technical analysis that occurs when a short-term moving average crosses above a long-term moving average, typically the 50-day SMA crossing above the 200-day SMA. This indicates a potential shift from a downtrend to an uptrend, often prompting traders to consider **buying** opportunities.

A **death cross** is a technical analysis pattern indicating a potential shift from a bullish to a bearish market trend. It occurs when a short-term moving average (typically the 50-day SMA) crosses below a long-term moving average (typically the 200-day SMA) on a price chart. This crossover is seen as a **bearish** signal, suggesting a downtrend.

Fig. 5.33 Technical analysis indicators

Be careful when using this method. It offers no guarantee of always being correct!

To preserve our previous work and reduce the load on the API, we'll now store all data in a **SQLite** database.

It is important to follow the process carefully, as it consists of two key steps.

Step 1: First, we create the **SQLite database** and initialize it by writing the data of a single stock into a table using the **DB Writer** node. This step is performed **only once**, as it sets up the structure of the stocks table.

Step 2: In all subsequent runs, we use the **DB Merge** node to insert only new stock data. This ensures that only records for stocks and dates not already present in the table are added.

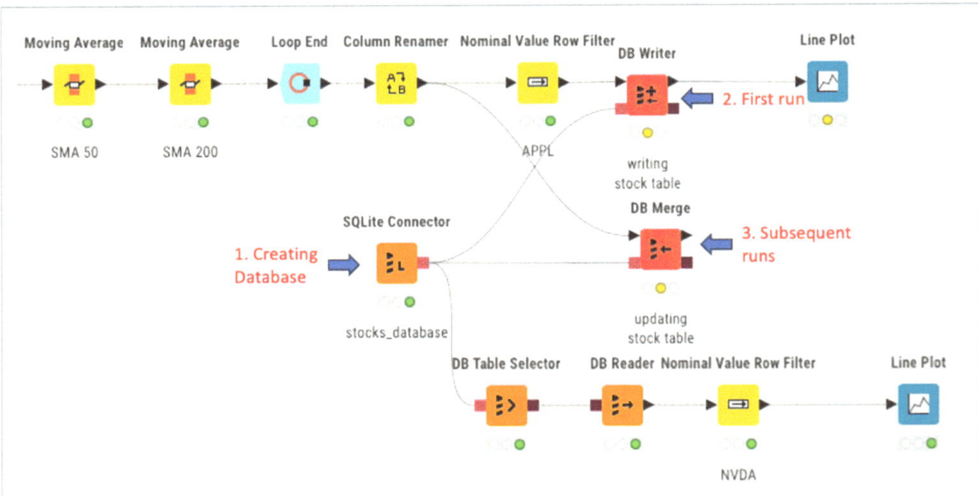

Fig. 5.34 Storing data in SQLite database

We can now query the database for the desired stocks, visualize their performance, and explore various indicators and trading strategies for further analysis.

5. Sports Analytics: Predicting Football Results with KNIME

Sports tournaments always include an amount of randomness which is hard to predict. This is especially true for soccer matches.

Nevertheless, the stronger team should win more often than not, as skill tends to outweigh luck over time. This raises the question: which indicators best capture a team's true strength? Are points achieved the most reliable measure, or do more detailed statistics like goal difference, expected goals, or shot quality provide a better signal of underlying performance?

To analyze this, we will attempt to predict the outcomes of matches in the second half of last season's **English Premier League** using only information available at mid-season: the total points each team had accumulated and their goal difference (i.e., the difference between goals scored and conceded).

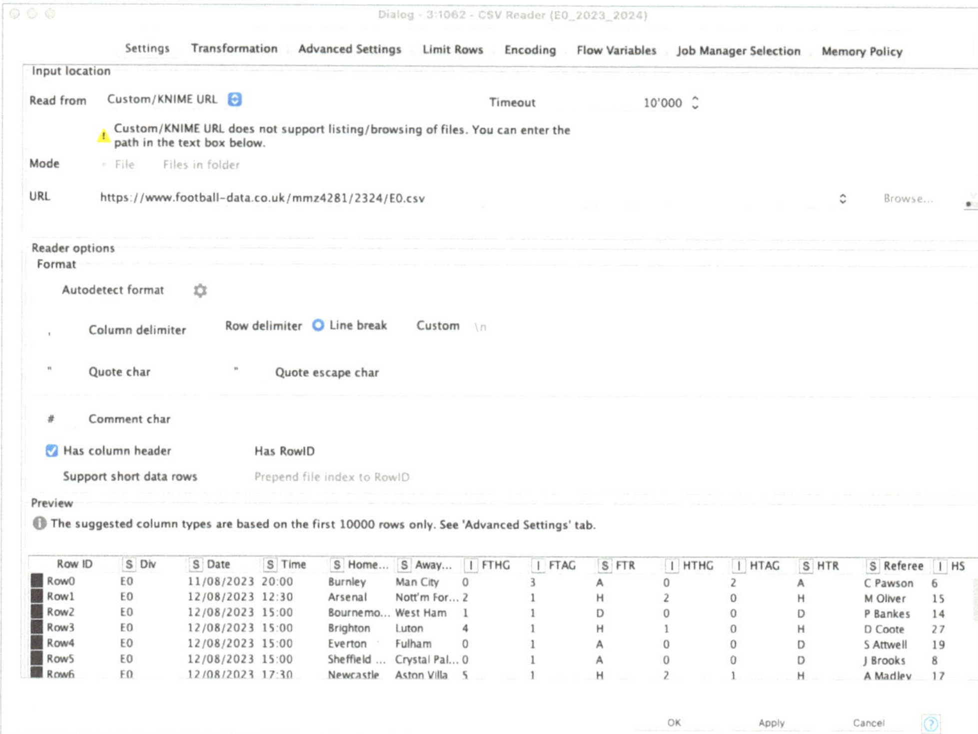

Fig. 5.35 Importing games from the English Premier League

By examining how well each of these metrics correlates with performance in the latter half of the season, we can evaluate which serves as a more reliable indicator of a team's underlying strength.

For this analysis, we will use the well-known dataset provided by the website football-data.co.uk, a popular and widely cited source for historical football statistics.

Let's jump straight into the match data. With the **CSV Reader** node we can directly import the games with the URL link provided on the site.

The first step is to construct a league table based on the first half of the season, recording each team's accumulated points as well as goals scored and conceded up to that point. In the next phase, we will merge these values with the data from the second half of the season and attempt to forecast the remaining matches.

Although the dataset provides match results, we still need to calculate the total points each team earned in order to build the league table. Therefore, we create a **Metanode** in which columns for the game number, season half, and points earned are generated.

In KNIME, a **Metanode** is used to organize and simplify workflows by grouping nodes, but it's not reusable or configurable. A **Component**, on the other hand, is modular and reusable, with defined input/output ports and a configuration dialog. Metanodes aid clarity; Components support reuse and sharing.

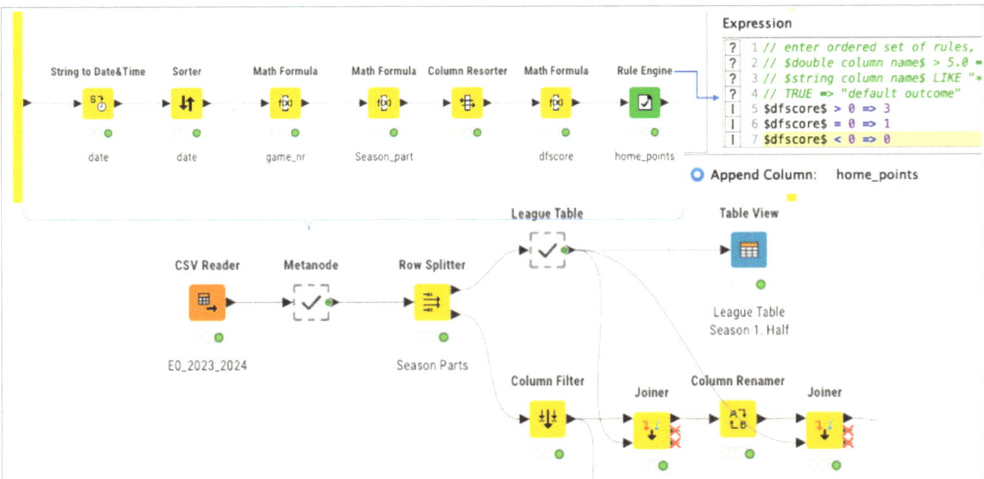

Fig. 5.36 Calculating earned points with **Rule Engine** node

For this, we use one of my first favorite nodes in KNIME: the **Rule Engine** node. This node allows us to determine the number of points earned in a match based on rules: 3 points for a win, 1 point for a draw, and 0 points for a loss.

In the second Metanode, we construct the league table by separately grouping home and away games to sum each team's points, goals scored, and goals conceded. We then join these two tables and calculate the total points, and scoring difference for each team. This completes the creation of our league table for the first half of the season.

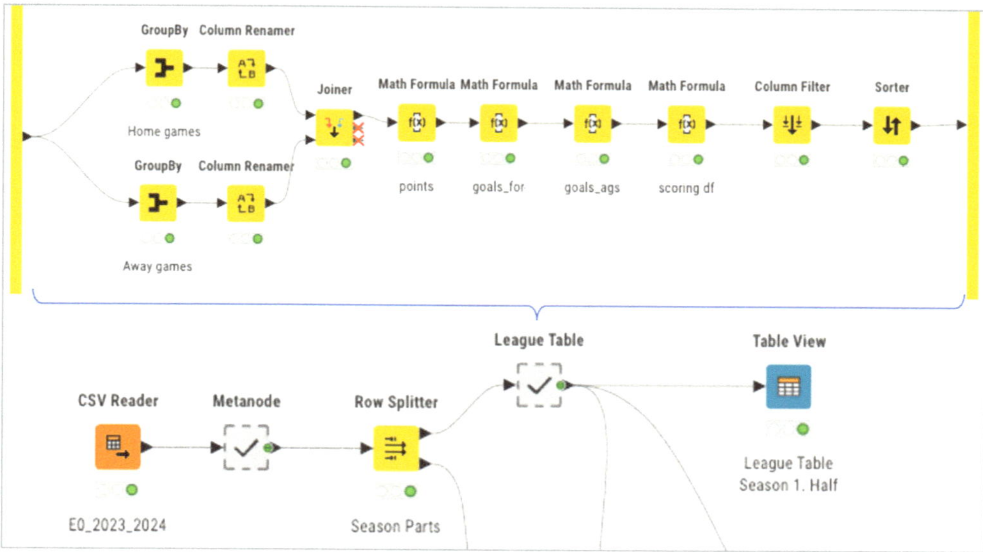

Fig. 5.37 Calculating the first half season league table

The future champions, Manchester City, were in fourth place at mid-season with 37 points. However, a closer look reveals that their scoring difference was 22, placing them just behind Liverpool in terms of overall scoring strength.

#	Team String	points Number (Integer)	goals_for Number (Integer)	goals_ags Number (Integer)	scoring df Number (Integer)
1	Liverpool	42	39	16	23
2	Aston Villa	42	43	27	16
3	Arsenal	40	36	18	18
4	Man City	37	43	21	22
5	Tottenham	36	39	28	11
6	West Ham	33	33	30	3
7	Man United	31	21	25	-4

Fig. 5.38 Half-season league table

At first glance, scoring difference seems to provide a stronger indication of team performance than the total points earned.

In fact, the correlation between scoring difference and the outcome of a match is slightly higher (0.499) than the correlation based on points difference (0.428).

The mean point difference is 6.56 for a home win, -1.0 for a draw, and -8.3 for an away win. For scoring difference, the values are 10.36 for a home win, -1.4 for a draw, and -13.44 for an away win.

Now, how can we build a prediction system using these values?

One way to make predictions is by setting cutoff points based on the mean differences. These cutoffs help define the boundaries for forecasting a home win, draw, or away win.

By analyzing last season's English championship, we observe that approximately 24% of matches ended in a draw, 46% resulted in home wins, and 30% in away wins. These percentages will serve as a basis for determining an appropriate threshold to help us make match predictions based on scoring differences.

We found that 25% of the scoring differences fall within the range of -8 to 6, which aligns closely with the proportion of drawn matches. Therefore, the optimal threshold for this championship is set between -8 and 6.

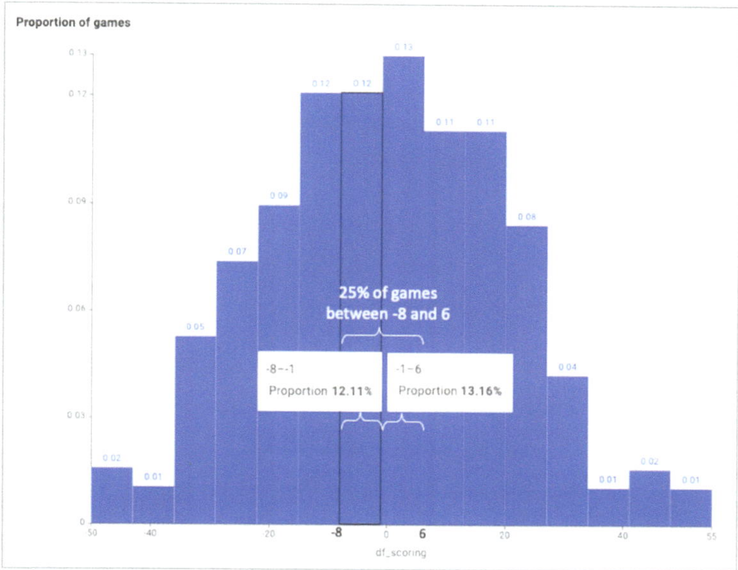

Fig. 5.39 Defining the threshold for scoring difference

We apply this using a **Rule Engine** node, which determines whether our prediction is a home win, draw, or away win based on the scoring difference of the two playing teams.

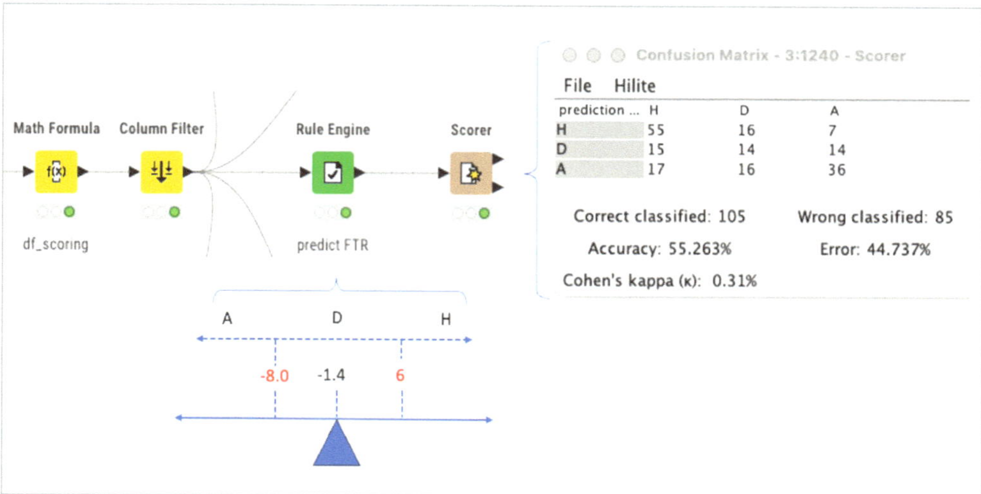

Fig. 5.40 Prediction of Game Outcomes and Accuracy Rates

Home advantage is a well-known factor in football. As we observed earlier, about 46% of Premier League matches end in a home win. Therefore, simply predicting a home victory in every match would result in an average accuracy of 46%.

By contrast, our rating system, based on the thresholds we have defined, achieves a prediction accuracy exceeding 55%. Not bad for a start!

But maybe we could do even better. After all, our ratings are based only on the results from the first half of the season. If we also took recent games into account, our forecasts might improve.

This could be achieved by iterating through each week and updating the league table after each round. Over the long run, updating points and goal differences alone would tend to flatten out, as teams' values converge toward an average. A more responsive rating system that adapts more rapidly to changes in performance could provide better insights.

The **Elo rating** system, for example, adjusts team ratings after each match by taking into account not only the outcome, but also the relative strength of the two teams. When a weaker team beats a stronger one, its rating increases more, while the stronger team's rating decreases. If the expected result occurs, rating changes are smaller. This makes Elo quick to reflect recent performance shifts.

We could now start coding a routine in **Python** to calculate Elo ratings for the teams. But there's also a big shortcut: we can let **K-AI** handle everything for us.

K-AI is an AI-powered code generation engine in KNIME that can automatically generate Python code from natural language descriptions.

But that's not all it can do. It also helps with data analysis, transformation, and workflow automation by interpreting user intent.

After the **CSV Reader**, we insert a **Python Script** node, open it with a double-click, and simply tell K-AI what we want. (*Mind that you need to have a free account on the KNIME Community Hub for K-AI to work*):

> „Implement an Elo rating system for soccer matches.
> Account for match outcomes (win/draw/loss), home
> advantage, and goal difference using the World
> Football Elo scaling formula. Add each team's Elo
> rating before the match to the input table.»

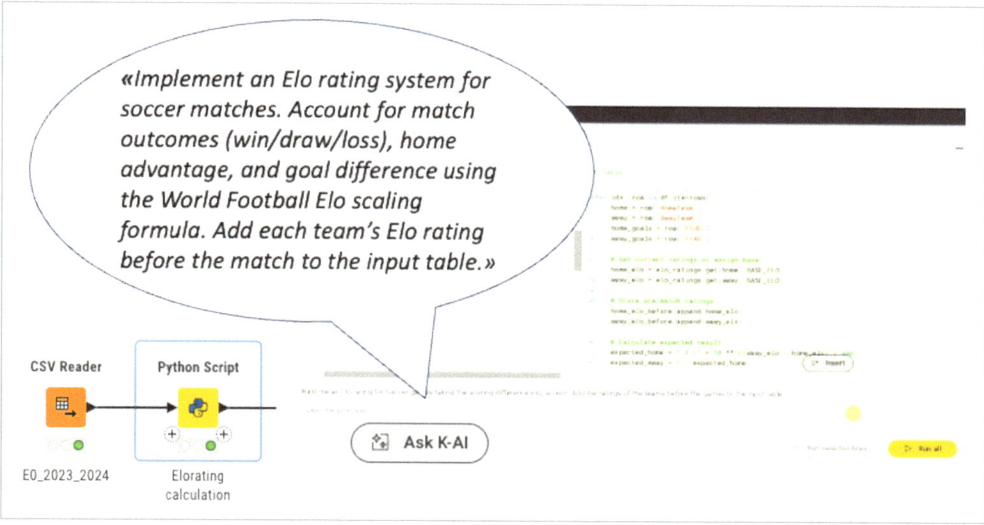

Fig. 5.41 Generating the Elo Rating Python code with **K-AI**

It takes a few seconds until the desired Python code is created. But the result is amazing.

If you take a closer look at the code, you will notice that all the necessary steps to calculate the corresponding Elo ratings have been implemented correctly.

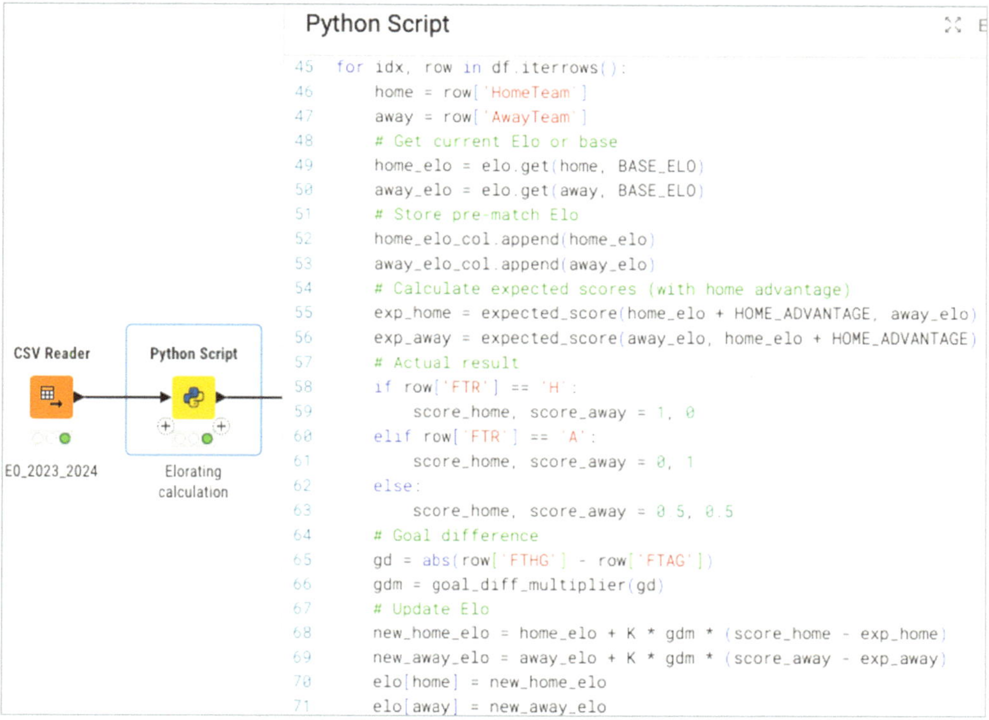

Fig. 5.42 Elo rating code in Python

When using K-AI in KNIME to generate Python code, it's important to be aware that the output may vary between prompt submissions, even when the input prompt remains the same. This variability is due to the generative nature of large language models, which can produce multiple valid responses based on the same instruction.

While this can be useful for exploring different solutions, it may require saving the output or refining prompts for more consistent results.

With K-AI, we have taken the first step on an exciting new journey. One where code writes itself and ideas flow faster than ever. What lies ahead promises to be even more powerful, creative and accessible.

Time for the next example. It's where data meets design, and where numbers begin to tell a story - quite literally on a map.

6. Visualization with K-AI & Python: Recreating Minard's Chart

Charles Joseph Minard's map of **Napoleon's** lost campaign in Russia in 1812 is probably one of the best charts ever created and it is considered one of the most influential examples of data visualization in history.

Minard created this diagram of Napoleon's Russian campaign in 1869, revolutionizing data visualization over 150 years ago. Unlike traditional charts that focus solely on one data dimension, Minard's diagram masterfully combines three elements: geography, time, and statistics into a coherent and fascinating narrative.

His map is easy to read and interpret, even for people who are not familiar with data visualization.

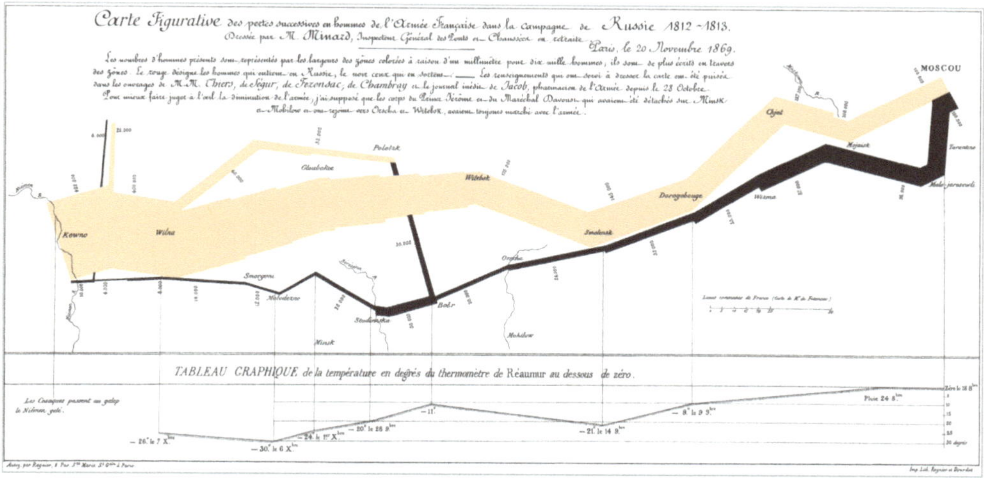

Fig. 5.43 Minard's map of Napoleon's Russian campaign of 1812

The width of the band in the chart represents the size of Napoleon's army at various points along its march. The journey begins in Kovno, Lithuania (on the left side of the image), where the army numbered 422,000 soldiers. It traces their advance to Moscow and the subsequent retreat during the brutal Russian winter. The dark lower band shows the return path, ending with only 30,000 survivors. This visual is also linked to temperature and timeline data shown at the bottom of the graphic.

Although Minard's chart is more than 150 years old, reproducing it using modern visualization tools like Tableau or Power BI remains a challenge. Creating it in Python requires a deep understanding of libraries such as

Matplotlib. However, with the support of KNIME's K-AI, we can still accomplish this effectively. So let's dive in. In the previous chapter, we saw just how powerful K-AI can be.

Before we start building the chart, we need to understand the dataset. Fortunately, it's available across several platforms. A list of the different formats can be found here:

https://www.datavis.ca/gallery/re-minard.php

LONC	LATC	CITY	LONT	TEMP	DAYS	MON	DAY	LONP	LATP	SURV	DIR	DIV
24	55	Kowno	37.6	0	6	Oct	18	24	54.9	340000	A	1
25.3	54.7	Wilna	36	0	6	Oct	24	24.5	55	340000	A	1
26.4	54.4	Smorgoni	33.2	-9	16	Nov	9	25.5	54.5	340000	A	1
26.8	54.3	Molodexno	32	-21	5	Nov	14	26	54.7	320000	A	1
27.7	55.2	Gloubokoe	29.2	-11	10	Nov	24	27	54.8	300000	A	1
27.6	53.9	Minsk	28.5	-20	4	Nov	28	28	54.9	280000	A	1
28.5	54.3	Studienska	27.2	-24	3	Dec	1	28.5	55	240000	A	1
28.7	55.5	Polotzk	26.7	-30	5	Dec	6	29	55.1	210000	A	1
29.2	54.4	Bobr	25.3	-26	1	Dec	7	30	55.2	180000	A	1
30.2	55.3	Witebsk						30.3	55.3	175000	A	1
30.4	54.5	Orscha						32	54.8	145000	A	1
30.4	53.9	Mohilow						33.2	54.9	140000	A	1
32	54.8	Smolensk						34.4	55.5	127100	A	1
33.2	54.9	Dorogobouge						35.5	55.4	100000	A	1
34.3	55.2	Wixma						36	55.5	100000	A	1
34.4	55.5	Chjat						37.6	55.8	100000	R	1
36	55.5	Mojaisk						37.5	55.7	98000	R	1
37.6	55.8	Moscou						37	55	97000	R	1
36.6	55.3	Tarantino						36.8	55	96000	R	1
36.5	55	Malo-jarosewli						35.4	55.3	87000	R	1
								34.3	55.2	55000	R	1
								33.3	54.8	37000	R	1
								32	54.6	24000	R	1
								30.4	54.4	20000	R	1
								29.2	54.4	20000	R	1
								28.5	54.3	20000	R	1
								28.3	54.4	20000	R	1

Fig. 5.44 Minard's dataset

The dataset is not a standard, flat CSV file. Instead, it has a unique and irregular structure. As you'll notice, it's not uniformly formatted. In fact, it essentially contains three separate tables combined into a single file:

- **Column 1–3**: longitude, latitude and names of cities
- **Column 4–8**: longitude, temperature, number of days on the retreat march and dates (during the march home only)
- **Column 9–13**: longitude, latitude, number of surviving troops, direction of travel (A=towards the attack/R=return journey) and division of army

The first thing to notice about Minard's map is that it's composed of three distinct layers: the top section displays city names, the middle illustrates the army's movement with line paths, and the bottom presents temperature data over time.

To recreate this visualization, we'll begin by splitting the dataset into these three components, build each graphic separately, and then combine them into a single, unified view.

K-AI will create this for us with the following prompt:

> The data comes from Minard's chart. Split the table into three parts:
>
> – a Cities dataset
>
> – a Temperature dataset
>
> – a Troops dataset
>
> Return each dataset as a separate output table.

After a while we get the following code:

Fig. 5.45 Generated Python Code for dividing dataset in three parts

When we execute this node in KNIME, we get an error. We must first create three output ports so that our files created in the **Python Script** node can be output.

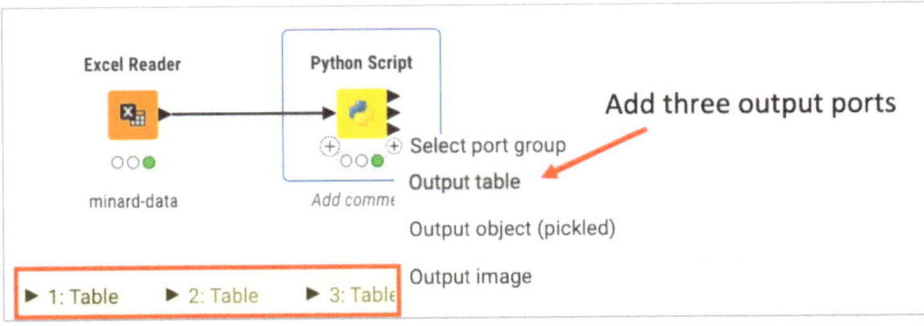

Fig. 5.46 Adding three output ports

After re-executing the node, we now see three output tables in the lower part. So let's create the first plot of the cities using their coordinates using the following prompt. For this, we'll use the **Python View** node, since we want a visual output. We'll prompt K-AI with the following instructions:

> "LONC is the x-axis value. LATC is the y-axis value. Draw a plot with the names of the cities in the column CITY."

We get the following code:

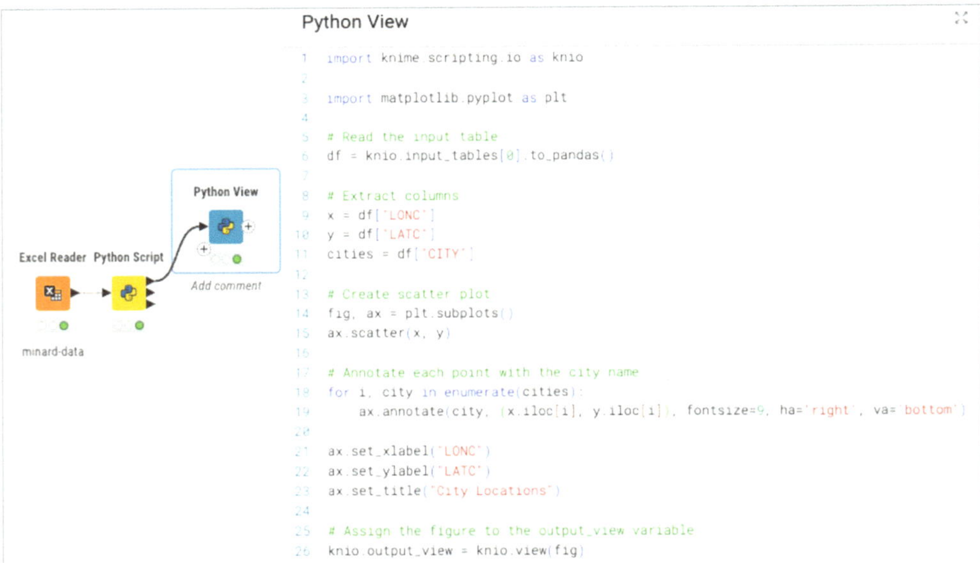

Fig. 5.47 Generated Python Code for creating city map

The Python View plots the cities according to their longitude and latitude values. The generated Python code creates a scatterplot with these coordinates.

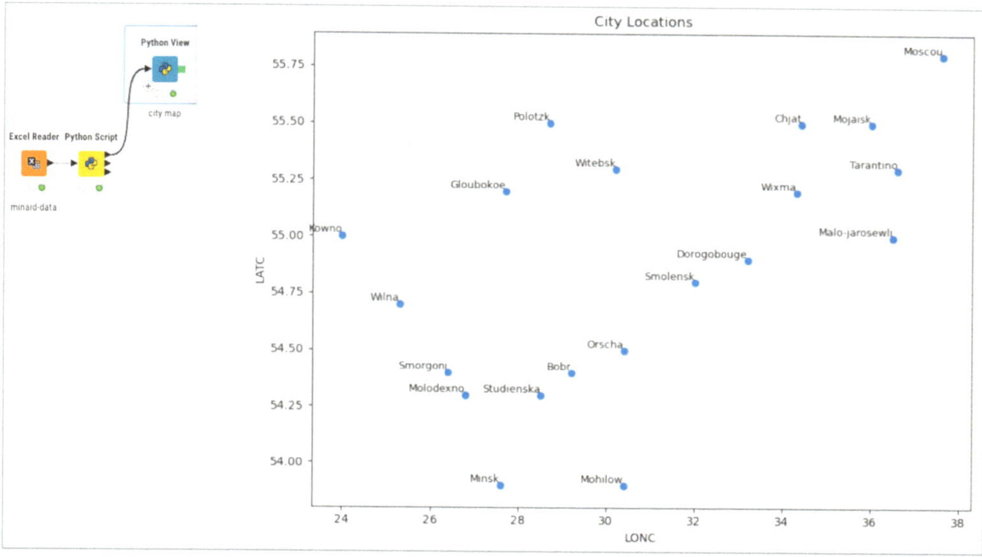

Fig. 5.48 Plot of the cities

However, geographical coordinates are not the same as x and y values, as they have a different scale. For this example, we will be satisfied with an approximation.

The second table generated by the Python script contains the temperature data recorded during Napoleon's troop march.

We use the following prompt to create the plot:

> „Draw me a dashed black line chart. LONT is on the x-axis, TEMP is on the y-axis. TEMP and DAY are integer values. Label the points with TEMP + MON + DAY. Add the degree symbol behind TEMP in the label."

The resulting chart visualizes temperature changes along the march route, with each point labeled by temperature (including the degree symbol), month, and day to provide detailed context for the data.

The original Minard chart includes three different temperature scales: Réaumur, Celsius, and Fahrenheit.

The chart displays temperatures in degrees Réaumur. For example, -30 degrees Réaumur is equivalent to -37.5 degrees Celsius or -34 degrees Fahrenheit. For details on converting between these temperature units, see the Wikipedia page on temperature conversion.

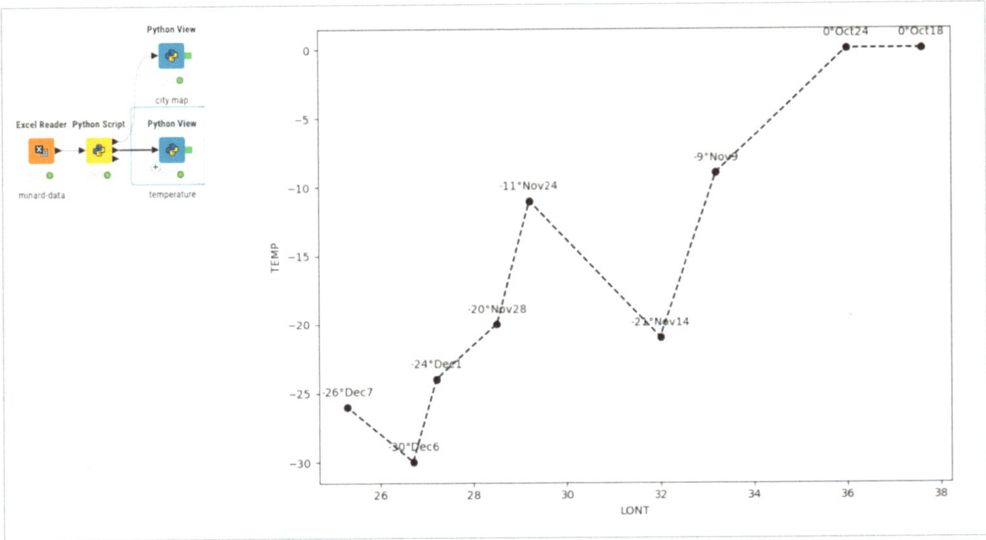

Fig. 5.49 Plot of the temperatures

The third table shows the positions of the troops during the march, how many survived at each point, the direction they were moving, and how the army was divided. Now, we create a line plot that shows the route of the march, where the thickness of the line reflects the number of surviving soldiers at each stage.

Let's prompt:

> "Create a line plot where LONP is the x-axis and LATP is the y-axis. Each point represents troop position. Connect the points in the order they appear in the data, without sorting. Use SURV to control the thickness of the line, where thicker lines represent more survivors."

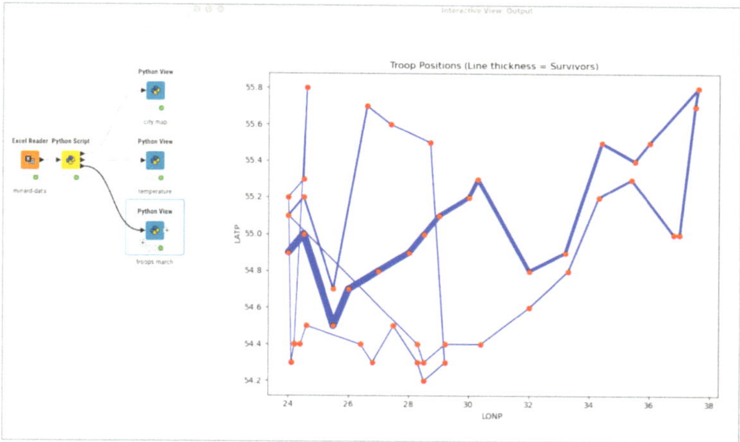

Fig. 5.50 Troops' March with line thickness indicating survivors

The result looks good, but we'd like to improve it by adjusting the line width to highlight the number of survivors. We also want to show the direction of the troops by using different colors for advance and retreat.

We tell K-AI to update the current chart with an additional instruction (using the color tan for the advancing troops, as in Minard's original map). We then prompt:

> "Color the line based on the column DIR: use tan when DIR is 'A', otherwise use black. Increase the line width so it is thicker but still proportional to the SURV column."

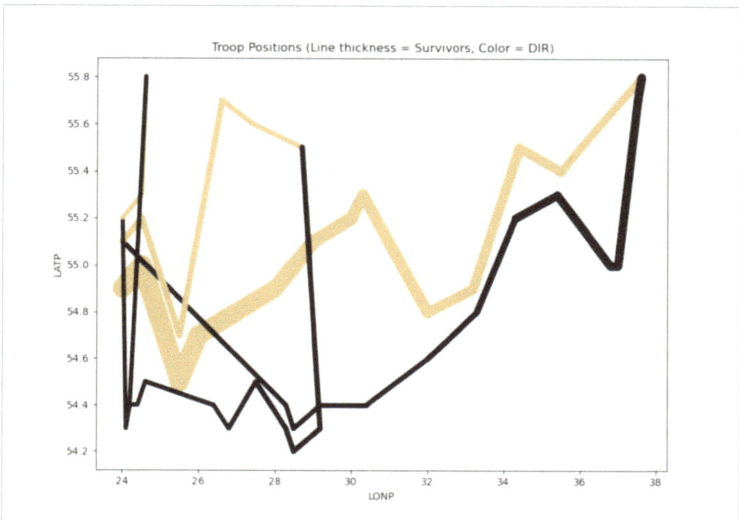

Fig. 5.51 Troops' March line showing direction by color

We loaded the Minard data file using an **Excel Reader** node, split it into three separate tables with a **Python Script** node, and then created the three different layers of the diagram with the **Python View** node.

Now, let's bring everything together. We combine all the prompts in a **Python View** node and proceed step by step by entering the following prompts one at a time in the K-AI interface:

> The data comes from Minard's chart. Split the table into three parts: a Cities part, a Temperature part, a Troops part
>
> Add a Chart:
>
> LONC is the x-axis value. LATC is the y-axis value. Draw a plot with the names of the cities in the column CITY.
>
> Add another Layer to the chart:
>
> Create a line plot where LONP is the x-axis and LATP is the y-axis. Each point represents troop position. Connect the points in the order they appear in the data, without sorting. Use SURV to control the thickness of the line, where thicker lines represent more survivors.
>
> Color the line based on the column DIR: use tan when DIR is 'A', otherwise use black. Increase the line width so it is thicker but still proportional to the SURV column.
>
> Add a Subplot half the height of the chart above:
>
> Draw me a dashed black line chart. LONT is on the x-axis, TEMP is on the y-axis. TEMP and DAY are integer values. Label the points with TEMP + MON + DAY. Add the degree symbol behind TEMP in the label.
>
> Adjust the x-axis so that LONC, LONP and LONT are on the same scale.
>
> Add in the temperature plot a horizontal grid
>
> Add the chart Title: "Napolean's Russian Campaign" with fontsize 30 and the subtitle "Figurative map of successive losses in men of the French army in the Russian campaign 1812" with fontsize 10

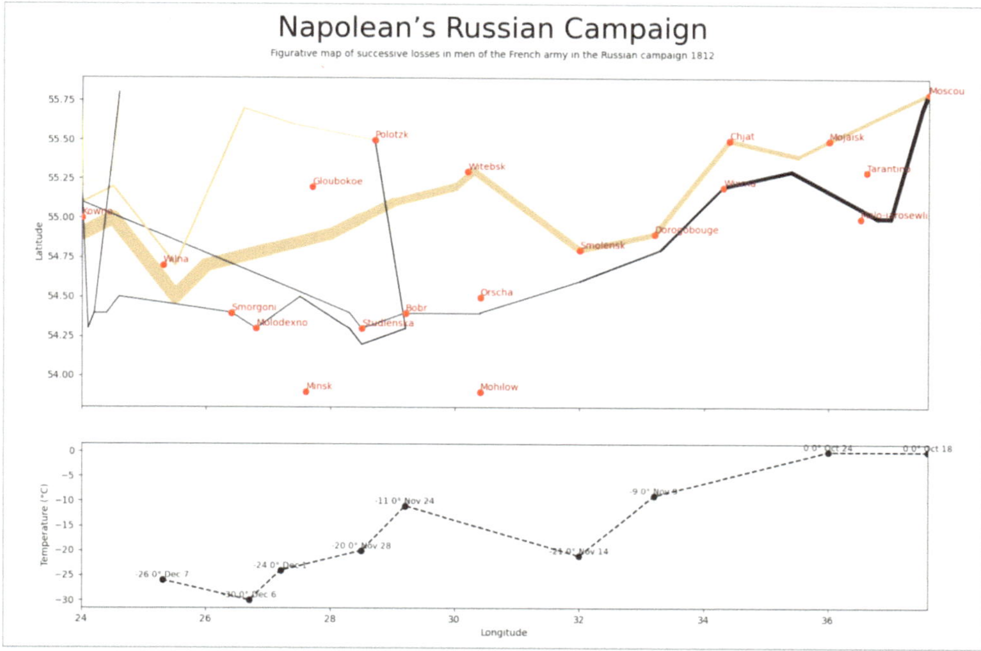

Fig. 5.52 The final Minard chart, created collaboratively using K-AI and Python.

Not bad! We were able to create the chart just by prompting our requests.

Prompting isn't exactly rocket science, but it does take some interaction and experimentation to get the results you want. Still, it's a fun and creative way to get your work done. Give it a try!

FINAL WORD

We have seen in the last chapter how KNIME can be applied to diverse, real-world scenarios, from everyday analytics to complex, creative data storytelling.

Visual programming languages like KNIME transform data science into an intuitive, visual language. Instead of just writing code, you build workflows by connecting nodes that tell a story and reveal insights. This approach makes complex data accessible, collaborative, and creative.

By embracing ***The KNIME Way***, you learn the language of visual data science and turn ideas into clear, powerful results. Keep building, keep exploring, and keep visualizing because the possibilities are endless.

Our journey is just beginning.

ABOUT THE AUTHOR

Dennis Ganzaroli is a senior data scientist with 25+ years of experience in analytics and data-driven strategy. He holds a Licentiate in Psychology and Computer Science from the University of Zurich (Switzerland). For over 14 years, Dennis has held leadership and analytics roles at Swisscom across both B2B and B2C divisions. He has led teams, developed innovative reporting solutions, and implemented advanced analytics strategies that have reduced costs, improved efficiency, and enabled smarter decision-making. His diverse background spans market research, business intelligence, and advanced analytics. Dennis also shares his expertise through engaging Medium articles that inspire both data professionals and business leaders.

linkedin.com / in / dennis-ganzaroli-17785222
x.com / DennisGanzaroli
youtube.com / @deganza11
amazon.com / stores / Dennis-Ganzaroli / author / B0FLWJ676C

www.ingramcontent.com/pod-product-compliance
Ingram Content Group UK Ltd.
Pitfield, Milton Keynes, MK11 3LW, UK
UKHW060018051026
15591UKWH00003B/263
* 9 7 9 1 2 2 4 3 0 8 0 3 4 *